PROMISE OF HOPE

COLONEL MARK COOK

PROMISE OF HOPE

With a Foreword by Martin Bell

HAMISH HAMILTON · LONDON

HAMISH HAMILTON LTD

Published by the Penguin Group
Penguin Books Ltd, 27 Wrights Lane, London w8 5tz, England
Penguin Books USA Inc., 375 Hudson Street, New York, New York 10014, USA
Penguin Books Australia Ltd, Ringwood, Victoria, Australia
Penguin Books Canada Ltd, 10 Alcorn Avenue, Toronto, Ontario, Canada m4v 3b2
Penguin Books (NZ) Ltd, 182–190 Wairau Road, Auckland 10, New Zealand

Penguin Books Ltd, Registered Offices: Harmondsworth, Middlesex, England

First published 1994
1 3 5 7 9 10 8 6 4 2

PICTURE ACKNOWLEDGEMENTS: All photographs are from
the private collection of the author, with the exception
of pages 17 and 18 © Colin Boyle, and pages 22, 23, and 24 © James Hawes

Typeset by Datix International Limited, Bungay, Suffolk
Printed in Great Britain by Clays Ltd, St Ives plc
Filmset in 11.5/14.5 pt Monophoto Baskerville

A CIP catalogue record for this book is available from the British Library
ISBN 0–241–13467–6

For Caroline

'Let this story shine like a bright light in dark and tragic times'

– *His Excellency Mr Bryan Sparrow, British Ambassador in Zagreb*

Contents

Foreword

In the chronicle of the wars of ex-Yugoslavia – which, sadly, are not yet over – the calamities of Bosnia have tended to overshadow the preceding conflicts, in Slovenia and Croatia. But they are all acts in the same continuing tragedy.

Most witnesses to the diplomacy agree that it was the European Community's decision, late in 1991, to proceed with the piecemeal recognition of Slovenia and Croatia that made the war in Bosnia inevitable. A deal done in Brussels left a doomed republic to be fought over, to the death, by its constituent peoples – with the Serbs, of course, leading the charge. And the seven-month Croatian war, which ended not with a peace but with a ceasefire, gave ample warning to the rest of Europe of what lay ahead if the Balkan conflagration remained unchecked.

Even to this day, in all the war zones of Bosnia there is no destruction more complete than that which the Serbs visited on the Croatian town of Vukovar, which they turned into a Stalingrad on the Danube. A Serbian colonel told me at the time, not just as a matter of record but of pride, that they hit it with two million shells.

Lipik was another and lesser-known example. An old spa town in central Croatia, it had the misfortune to lie on the ethnic fault line, and therefore the front line, between Serbs and Croats. When the fighting started, the Serbs destroyed Lipik totally. The more substantial buildings were particular targets – and these included the hundred-year-old orphanage, whose children were saved by its cellar.

It was some time after this that Colonel Mark Cook of the Gurkha Rifles, discovering the rubble almost by chance, happened upon the mission that would transform his life. It was hardly a career move on his part – indeed, he left the army shortly afterwards. But he didn't choose the cause: the cause chose him. He was at the time commander of all British UN troops in ex-Yugoslavia, and a busy man with responsibilities from Split to Sarajevo. But he took it upon himself to rebuild the orphanage, against odds so daunting that if he had really known what they were he might not even have started.

My own part in the project was marginal, and not at all deliberate. Mark had come to Sarajevo four months into the Bosnian war and at a particularly dangerous time. His task was to assess the dangers faced by a troop of Royal Engineers, who were occupied in providing protection for others while receiving little themselves. But the orphanage was also much on his mind, and he sought me out in the belief that with my media contacts I might somehow be able to raise funds for it. I was about to point out that in the matter of financial acumen I was probably more of a liability than an asset and certainly no use as a fund-raiser. But an event which then occurred proved me quite wrong. It was one of a series of coincidences and connections that enabled Mark to embark on his Mission Impossible.

Within eighteen months more than a million pounds had been raised; and the orphanage had not only been rebuilt in the original Austro-Hungarian style, but greatly improved as well. Then, one day in December, the children returned to it, hugging their benefactor – by then an ex-soldier with tears of joy in his eyes. Nothing in a successful military career could ever compare with that moment.

This book is the story of what he did and how he did it – and also of the coincident turmoil in his private life, which he sets out with great candour. It was an episode that introduced him, for the first time and to his great dismay, to the nether world of journalism – the tabloids and their sliding scale of news values. But his zeal and his success were unaffected. And the celebrity that he never sought surely helped him to raise the money.

I am often asked, since I hang about the Balkan war zones more than is good for my health, whether I am by now a total pessimist about them, and indeed about the human condition in general. The answer is no. There are two things that strike me about those places. The first is that, for all the supposed emotive power of television, the words and images do not exist that can adequately convey the reality of what is happening there and the sufferings of ordinary people. The second is that the death and destruction of which we provide everyday accounts are the setting – perhaps even the *condition* – for the most extraordinary acts of courage and heroism by those who light a candle in that darkness.

Mark Cook is one of those people. His work has shown – and his words proclaim – what a difference one man can make.

Martin Bell
July 1994

Introduction

Some people may ask why I have chosen to write this book. The idea was first suggested to me at the very outset of a series of events that took place over a period of eighteen months and completely changed my life. By the end the BBC had decided to make a film, and several publishers had asked me to write a book. Initially they all envisaged that it would be concerned solely with the rebuilding of the ruined orphanage in Lipik, Croatia, but then they realized that there was more involved and I was persuaded to write the story in full. This has been particularly difficult and hurtful for my wife, Caroline, as I have spent the last six months recording the past. My hope is that this will act as a cathartic process.

Having seen their shattered home in Lipik and heard of their terrifying ordeal, I made a promise to the children who used to live there and to their doctor, Marina Topić, that I would rebuild it for them. The children, about seventy in all, had little but the security of the home before the war and now they had lost that too. They had no family to love and look after them and virtually no hope of a happy and normal life.

On many occasions during the eighteen months it took to fulfil my promise, the practical problems and emotional complications seemed overwhelming. Then I would look at photographs of the children and know that, whatever the cost, I had to carry on. I was sustained in this period by the love and understanding of many wonderful friends and the support of so many people that only a few can be mentioned in this book. But I would like to thank them all, literally hundreds of people around the world, who sent me letters, money and aid. The proof of their generosity and kindness is manifestly evident in the beautiful pink buildings that are now home for eighty young, innocent victims of the horrifying war in the Balkans.

The reconstruction of the orphanage in Lipik became a symbol of hope to the people in a wide area whose own homes and lives had been shattered in the war. It provided employment for 160 local men for seven months, and all the materials used came from within Croatia. It was, therefore, an injection of £1 million into the local economy.

If there is one word that can encapsulate the whole project, it is *hope*. When people have lost everything and when children are made orphans, the one thing they need more than anything else is hope: hope that they will get warmth, water, food, medicine, clothing and a roof over their heads. They can only hope that things will get better. They rely on the hope that there are enough good people in the world, better off than they are, who care enough to do something to help them in their plight. They live in hope; if they lose this and it turns to despair, they die.

So many people in the world do care, and these are the people who enabled me to keep my promise. Never once did I doubt that the money would come from somewhere, and from an early stage I became aware that I was having too many strokes of good luck for these to be put down as mere coincidence.

The chaos, death and destruction that some people seem intent on creating in the world bring out the best qualities in others. Love, kindness and understanding can prevail over sin and evil.

I

The Attack on Lipik

All the children were asleep when the shell landed on the orphanage roof. The explosion reverberated through the thick walls which had stood for a hundred years, providing a sanctuary and a home for many thousands of children who had nothing else in life.

The shell was the opening shot of the war on Lipik, a pretty, small town between Zagreb and Belgrade, and it was followed by many more as the children were startled into wakefulness and fear, jumping from their beds to see what was happening. Was it a thunderstorm? An earthquake? What could be shaking their world so suddenly? Fear gripped the older ones first because they were more aware of the political tensions around their home town, which had been threatening for some months to become full-scale war. They had heard the grown-ups talking in the bars and cafés and shops around the orphanage, telling tales of the dreadful things that were going on elsewhere in the countryside and which could soon be happening here. For the four- and five-year-olds it was more a question of puzzlement and confusion as they tried to make sense of what was happening to them.

The teacher on night duty, who had been dozing in the office downstairs in the adjoining building, knew immediately what the noise meant: the Serbs in the hills surrounding the town had decided that the time was right to begin the destruction of Lipik. He ran out into the courtyard and opened up the doors to both buildings as the wide-eyed and panic-stricken children came tumbling down the staircases wanting to know what they should do.

'The basement!' he shouted to them. 'Go down into the

cellar!' As the first ones ran down the steps there were more explosions outside and the teacher dashed up into the bedrooms to check that everyone was out. Every bed was empty, the covers tangled and soft toys left on the pillows. It was the summer holidays, August 1991, so half of the eighty inmates of the building were away staying with families, but there were still thirty-five heads to be accounted for.

A couple of the little ones had been left behind and had become too frightened to move. They were cowering in the corner, whimpering softly as their teacher came in. He scooped them up in his arms and carried them down into the gloomy basement where the older children were already cuddling the little ones, trying to comfort them and calm their cries. It was warm down there, with all the pipework from the boilers running along the walls and ceilings, and very dark. Stanko, a five-year-old Croatian orphan and the youngest of six children, took Bric the orphanage dog down with him, hugging him close.

Goran Nikles, the Acting Director of the children's home, lived in the next village, Pakrac, just two miles away. Pakrac came under attack from the Serbian guns in the hills at the same time as Lipik and was also suffering from heavy hand-to-hand street fighting. Intense machine-gun fire outside his flat woke Goran up, and he could hear the artillery in the background. The Serbs were trying to capture the police station, the symbol of local power. Goran, though only a young man himself, took his responsibilities for the children very seriously. The previous Director had recently left the job after many years, and while the authorities looked around for someone new, Goran had been asked to take temporary charge of the home. He had been a teacher there for some years and knew all the children well. When the shelling started he was torn between his urge to get to the children's home and make sure they were all right and his desire to stay to protect his wife, Gordana, and their own small children, Sven and Hrvoje. Gordana, a quietly spoken doctor, could see the anxiety on her husband's face and squeezed his hand. 'You must go and make sure they are all right. You can take me to the hospital, and the children to my parents.'

In retrospect it was a crazy thing to do, but the whole world seemed to be going mad outside and Goran felt he had to get into Lipik to see what was happening. Out in the street they ran to the car. There were armed men everywhere, dodging from corner to corner, firing at one another as the sky lit up with tracer bullets and the streets with the occasional flashes of shells exploding.

With his foot to the floor, Goran drove the road to Lipik in record time, having dropped the children, then Gordana at the hospital in Pakrac, which was still relatively unscathed at that stage. Arriving at the orphanage, he left the car on the forecourt and ran down to the basement to find the children and their teacher.

For the next ten days the Serbs kept up the bombardment and the children lived by candlelight in the cellars. Whenever there was a lull in the firing they would venture up to the lavatories or to get supplies, and would dodge back to the basement as soon as the shells began to rain down again. The teachers would accompany them to the lavatories to make sure they did not use too much of the precious water they were storing. In the weeks before the attack, when tension in the area had been mounting, Goran had been stockpiling food where he could, and had installed a calor gas cooker in one of the corners of the cellar so that he could produce meals of some sort, normally just soup and bread which he was able to bake himself. He had also filled one room with mattresses and brought down card games and comics which the children could amuse themselves with by the light of the candles or when enough daylight filtered in through the few narrow windows. Throughout the long, beautiful summer days, when the children should have been running around their playground and the adjoining park, they huddled underground and waited for the enemy to make his next move.

3

Daniel and Vladek, the seven-year-old Croatian twins, had to share a bed. Daniel was a sickly child; he had been a blue baby with a heart problem and was frightened of the dark at night. Every night he would fall out of the narrow bed and have to be comforted back to sleep. Vladek, on the other hand, was angelically serene, never appearing frightened or crying, just patient and smiling peacefully.

Every evening Goran would venture out on his own in search of fresh food and go to the Croat headquarters in a house nearby for news. A number of houses had already been hit, and some of the local families had come knocking on the orphanage door asking if they could shelter with the children as the cellars looked like the safest place in town. Goran found himself unable to turn them away, but he felt uneasy. The more people who knew the children were in the cellars, the more likely it was that the Serbs would find them and kill them when they eventually came down into the town. Everyone was a potential informer and enemy, even people who had been living in the surrounding streets all their lives. No one knew who to trust any more.

Everyone had heard tales of the atrocities which were being committed by Serbian troops when they came into Croatian towns, and no one hesitated to pass the stories on. 'Many people hide in their cellars because of the shells and mortars,' Goran was told one evening, 'but when the soldiers come in they don't bother to ask who is where, they just throw their grenades through the basement windows and blow everyone up.'

'They are raping and murdering everyone,' someone else told him. 'It would be better if they killed the children with a grenade than if they took them out and slaughtered them after having their way.'

The more Goran heard, the more certain he was that he should find a way to get the children out of the town before the troops arrived. But where to? And how would he transport them? Everyone left in the town knew that they were down there, there would be no chance that the attackers would miss them, and judging from stories which were coming in from other towns, there was little chance that their lives would be spared either.

Daniel's screams one afternoon brought Goran running from the kitchen end of the cellar. He had seen the figure of a man at one of the ground-level windows. The man was throwing something up against the wall. Goran held Daniel tightly and comforted him, explaining that it was local militia piling up sandbags against the windows. That was the last of the daylight blocked out.

One night Goran was given some news. 'There is a school in Bjelovar,' he was told, 'which is quiet at the moment because the children are on holiday. We will find a bus and take your children up there.'

So, ten days after the first shell fell, the children slipped quietly out of Lipik in a coach during the quiet hours of the early morning, and headed a few miles north to a town which was still untouched by violence. Goran, his family and the orphans managed to live there peacefully for a while: the children were able to get outside into the fresh air again and run around to stretch their muscles, which were aching with inactivity. But not for long. A month later the school holidays were over and the citizens of Bjelovar wanted their school back. News was coming in that the bombardment of Lipik had abated. It seemed that the Serbs felt they had achieved their objective and were turning their attentions elsewhere. There was a lot of damage at the orphanage, with the windows blown out and the walls peppered with shrapnel, but the structure of the buildings was still sound. Goran worried about what to do for several days. He rang his direct superior, who was based in Zagreb, a city which had managed to stay clear of any damage.

'We have heard nothing from Lipik,' he was told. 'It should be safe for you to go back.' In fact the reason why they had heard nothing in Zagreb was that the media were being strictly controlled by the Government. Goran had no one else to consult and no one to turn to for help. Since he had nowhere else to take them, he decided that the children would have to go back to the orphanage. It took some time to persuade a bus driver to take them back, but eventually he agreed, and the children returned to their scarred home, hoping to restart their lives. It was the worst possible decision.

Two days after the children's return the Serbs redoubled their efforts of destruction. They hurled shells down on the town twice as hard as before and the children fled back down into the blackness of the cellars. Having little else to do, they took to counting the explosions outside and on several days they counted over a thousand. For ten days they never left the cellar, using it as a kitchen, bedroom and bathroom because there was no let-up in the bombardment. One day Gordana, who had moved in with the children, was lying on a mattress when a shell went off directly outside, blowing the last remaining window in on top of her, despite the piles of sandbags, as she rolled over to protect her two-year-old, Sven, who was lying beside her.

During one particularly frightening bombardment Bric the dog panicked and bit Stanko, who was hugging him too hard for mutual comfort. The bite was a bad one, leaving a chunk of Stanko's thigh hanging off. Goran could see that he had to have medical attention and went outside as the mortars continued to fall, to ask for help getting the boy to the hospital in Pakrac.

One of the local militia listened to the story. 'You're mad,' he said. 'You can't take a child to Pakrac through all this.'

'Come and look at his leg.' Goran showed the man Stanko's wound and the soldier realized that he had to be treated. While Goran held the screaming boy, the soldier drove the car, hunched over the wheel and weaving through the streets to avoid the shell craters. Stanko was beside himself with fear and pain, fighting against Goran as he tried to hold him still.

Once the wound was sewn up they had to make the return journey along the same route.

Outside the orphanage the local population was now fleeing in large numbers. The children could not see what was happening, but they were virtually the only people left in Lipik, apart from a handful of residents who had not yet managed to find a way out. There were also thirty-five able-bodied men who had volunteered to stay on and defend the town against the might of the Serbian army, which was now poised to come down out of the hills and destroy everything it came across. These men knew that they were the only chance the town had of surviving. If they could hold on long enough, perhaps the United Nations or some other outside force would come to their aid. They couldn't possibly win if the Serbs attacked, but they might be able to delay them just long enough.

Goran could see as clearly as anyone that the army could walk in any day and they would then be completely at the mercy of the soldiers. The time had come to make another run for it, however dangerous it might be and however unknown their destination. Under the cover of darkness he went in search of the few men left in Lipik. He found some of them at the bar in Jura's café in the centre of town. They were drinking and talking, ignoring the constant crash of explosions in the streets outside. As Goran came in through the door the men looked at him suspiciously. He was not one of them. He was an educated, professional man, a family man who kept himself to himself and did not participate in village social life. They knew that he was doing a good job protecting the orphans, but that did not mean they had to trust him completely.

Goran didn't like having to throw himself on their mercy, but he had no alternative. 'I have to get the children out,' he said.

'You should never have brought them back here,' he was told. 'It was a bad mistake.'

'I know that now. But I must still get them out.'

As the evening wore on, the harassed Acting Director managed to persuade a man with a lorry to transport the children out of town at dawn. The firing was usually at its lightest then, perhaps because the soldiers were sleeping off their hangovers from their night's activities. Goran still had his car hidden at the back of the building and could use it to get his wife and children out at the same time. The man promised to be there. Goran set Milka, one of the older girls, to sewing a Red Cross flag to go on the side of the lorry.

Goran woke up before light the next morning and went out to get his car. Outside it was silent and dark. Everyone in the hills must have been asleep. Goran went round to the car and turned the key – nothing: the battery was completely flat. The lorry would be arriving any time now and the driver would be unwilling to hang around if Goran was not ready to leave.

He thought he remembered seeing a pile of batteries at the deserted filling station in town. He ran 500 yards to the garage and was rummaging through the debris when an enormous burst of mortar fire came crashing down from the hills around him. Looking around for cover, he saw a building which seemed to be holding firm and dived under it. The attack lasted for two long hours and Goran imagined the lorry driver giving up and going away. If they didn't get out today the chances were that there would be no vehicles left to take them. He felt as though his last chance was slipping away.

When it finally grew quieter he clambered out, grabbed a battery which he had spotted and ran back to the orphanage with it. The lorry was just arriving when he got there, but its arrival had been seen by other people, all of whom had come flocking round, clutching bags of their belongings, begging for lifts to safe areas. They all knew that this was almost certainly their last chance of survival.

Goran had to be firm. 'Children first,' he commanded, 'and

then if there is any room, others.' While they argued and pushed and jostled, he fitted the battery into his car and managed to start it.

When he went back to help the children into the lorry he noticed that the top and sides were very flimsy and would offer no protection against bullets. Summoning more strength than he knew he possessed, he began to swing sandbags which had been protecting the cellar windows up into the back of the lorry and piled them up along the sides. The children were then loaded in, none of them allowed to bring any possessions, nothing but themselves; all their precious toys had to be left on the steps of the nearest building. None of them protested; they were numbed and silenced by fear. Then some of the civilians were allowed to follow. Daniel stared, transfixed and shaking, at the wrinkled face of a frightened old woman lying opposite him.

The driver and Goran decided that the best way out of town was to head west to Kutina, even though that meant going along a stretch of road that was completely exposed to the guns and snipers in the hills.

'I suggest I go first,' the driver said, 'and you follow. Whatever happens, we keep going. We can't stop for anything or we will be sitting targets.' Goran nodded his agreement as he tried to quieten frightened children who were scuffling and scrabbling around in the bottom of the lorry beneath the sandbags.

The route out was going to take them past the glass factory, one of the town's major employers before the war, and the stables where they bred the famous white Lippizaner horses which perform at the riding school in Vienna. As they emerged from the town on to the most exposed section of the road, with the mortars once more falling out of the sky around them, they saw that the Lippizaner stables were on fire and the beautiful thoroughbred horses were running around in a crazed state on the road, making it impossible to keep going. They screeched to a halt and a rocket flew just behind the lorry, followed by another which skimmed under the car and exploded on the side of the road. The horses, completely wild with fear, eventually galloped off, and the two vehicles desperately tried to build up speed again to get back under the cover of a built-up area, out of the Serbs' sights.

By the time they arrived at Kutina, about 30 kilometres from Lipik, the children were in a state of hysteria, and it took Goran and Gordana nearly two hours to calm little Sven sufficiently to get him out of the car. Behind them the shells continued to pound down on Lipik, smashing their home seemingly beyond repair. Four days later the Serbs came down into the town and took it, destroying every remaining vestige of Croatian life. Like so many millions of people all over the world, I watched with horror the scenes of death and destruction shown on television. Little did I realize how closely involved my own life was to become with the fate of the children of Lipik.

2

Looking for Adventure

By the beginning of 1992 I was having serious doubts about whether I could go on with my life in the army much longer. I felt I had come to a point where I must look for new avenues if I was not to stagnate for the rest of my life. Having spent thirty years in service around the world, ending up commanding 6,500 men in Hong Kong, I was now back at Army Headquarters in Aldershot, shuffling papers around a desk with little apart from more boring staff jobs and a genteel retirement in a Wiltshire village to look forward to. It was beginning to look as if I was not going to be offered any more grand adventures, unless I went out looking for them myself.

My appointment was Deputy Chief of Staff in Headquarters Southern District and I had been there for two and a half dreary years. The people I was working with were delightful, but the actual work was stretching my patience to breaking point. There was a considerable threat from the IRA at that time, and I was responsible for the security of army personnel in Southern England, which was the interesting part of the job. It was also a time when the army was being reorganized, which meant that I had been caught up in the development of new management strategies and the devising of budget controls. I loathe things like charts, establishments, figures and money, and these were now taking up most of my time.

I believe that in order to do any job well your heart has to be in it, and mine was not in the piles of paper which were travelling back and forth across my desk every day. Because I knew that I was not doing a good job, I felt even more dissatisfied with my lot. I felt that I had wasted two and a half years of my life doing absolutely nothing productive. I was frustrated and getting depressed.

By the spring of 1992 I was beginning to do some serious thinking about my life so far and the years which were stretching ahead. I was approaching fifty, a milestone in anyone's life, and that was making me reflective. 'What if I was told that I had cancer and had only six months to live,' I asked myself one morning as I drove to work through the beautiful Wiltshire countryside. 'What have I achieved and, more importantly, what have I contributed to help others?'

I have had a very privileged life. I come from a comfortable family background and was privately educated at prep school and the Leys School in Cambridge, where I was able to indulge in as much sport as I wanted. I went on to Mons Officer Cadet School because I thought the army sounded like fun, and straight into the 1/10th Gurkha Rifles as a Second Lieutenant at the age of nineteen. The Gurkha regiments are very special, rather like a family, and I had been a part of that family for thirty years, working my way up until I ended up commanding the battalion at the age of forty. There were many British officers and Gurkhas who had been with me throughout my career and it had led to close ties and bonds and friendships. I had spent time doing virtually every job in the battalion and had enjoyed almost all of them. It had been a privileged and enjoyable life, but ultimately selfish. I didn't feel I had done much for my fellow man.

Once you have commanded a battalion you have to move on after two and a half years, and I had been very sad to leave the 10th Gurkhas. But I was fortunate again in that I was selected for promotion to Colonel and sent to Hong Kong to be Deputy Commander of the Gurkha brigade out there. In the last six months of my two and half years there the brigade split in two and I was given half of it to command (about 6,500 men). My job was to look after the logistic elements of the force, such as transport and engineering, helicopters and hospitals. I have always enjoyed being in command and I feel I am better at that than at being a staff officer dealing with paperwork.

I had also been extremely lucky in my private life. I have a wonderful wife, Caroline, who had patiently, and almost uncomplainingly, followed me around the world from posting to posting. In twenty-seven years we had lived in twenty different houses and she had had to put up with all the discomforts and inconveniences of being an army wife in places like Malaya, Hong Kong and Germany. We had two teenage sons of whom I was very proud: Edward, whom we adopted as a new-born baby, and William, who had been conceived a few months later. Although life in the army offers plenty of opportunity for adventure and new experiences, it can be very hard on families. Children like to have somewhere they can call home, however much they enjoy the excitement of being constantly on the move. We always seemed to be moving, having to find homes for family pets and saying goodbye to friends and people whom we had come to love. For the men there are the distraction and challenge of starting new jobs all the time, with ready-made friends, but the women and children are left constantly having to restart their lives in new houses among new people. Cars and many household things have to be bought again in different countries, new shops explored and new relationships built; it can be very stressful and unsettling, particularly for those wives who do not like such a nomadic life.

Caroline was a trained nanny when I first met her, and soon afterwards she placed an advertisement in a magazine saying, 'Young girl seeks employment in the sun'. As well as receiving a few unsavoury calls, she was approached by a widow with a young child who was trying to run a farm in the wilds of Kenya. When I said that I wanted to go out to visit her there she tried to put me off, as she did other boyfriends, saying that it was miles from anywhere with absolutely nothing to do, but I refused to be discouraged.

Emerging from a six-month operational tour in the jungle of Sarawak, fighting against the Indonesian army, I managed to hitch a lift to Nairobi with a friend on a Canadian Air Force plane. I then made my way up-country to the farm where Caroline was working and two weeks later we became engaged – I proposed in the swimming pool on the Amboseli Game Reserve. We married in Wiltshire; the reception was held on the immaculate lawns of Caroline's lovely family home. I was probably too young and inexperienced to embark on marriage, but I did not think so at the time. The army and then the children swept our lives forward.

Now, after twenty-five years, we felt we had finally come home to some peace and quiet. We had owned a home in Britain for many years, but it was not large enough for us to move into full-time, so we sold up and went house-hunting. Caroline had very fixed ideas of what she wanted: something Georgian, with light, gracious rooms, in the same style as her parents' house. We looked at several which were not suitable and then went to view the Mill House in Steeple Langford, near Salisbury. The village was tiny and quiet, with pretty grey brick houses clustered in the valley of the River Wylye. The river ran just ten feet away from the front door of the Mill House, which had a garden room built across it. The house looked out over the river, with its little wooden bridges, across the gardens to the water meadows beyond. It was my dream house.

As we got back into the car, Caroline chucked the details on to the back seat. 'Another one for the bin,' she announced disappointedly.

'Oh no,' I protested, 'don't you see, that's the one. It's perfect. It's just what we need.'

'No, I don't like it.' She looked taken aback by my enthusiasm. 'It's too long and thin.'

'I tell you what,' I suggested, 'we'll bring the boys to see it and take a family vote.' I knew I was on safe ground here because William is a fanatical fisherman, so being next to a river would be his idea of heaven, and I was just as confident that Edward would like it.

'All right,' Caroline sighed, knowing that she was beaten.

Life in Steeple Langford is much as it must have been for the last couple of centuries. There were already two generals, two majors, an air commodore and a squadron leader in the village, and with my arrival there were two colonels as well. To start with, I couldn't wait to get into the heart of village life, eagerly awaiting my turn to be a sidesman at the church next to the house. It seemed that my future was mapped out. I was recruited into the British Legion and would parade with the others, all wearing our medals, every year on Remembrance Sunday. I would play a role in the organization of the local village fête. I would attend all the right cocktail parties in the right houses. I would wear tweed suits and keep up appearances under the watchful eyes of the general who lived on the hill above us, and had been commanding the village for many years. He lost no time in telling me he had lined me up to take over a number of duties from him when the time was ripe. It was the sort of life I had always imagined we would lead when I retired, particularly when we were living in the steam and bustle of the Far East and dreaming about the quiet rural life in beautiful old Britain. I was all set to become what is called in the army an old 'Curry Puff' or 'Colonel Blimp', walking the dog at the same time each day and writing strong letters of protest about everything to newspapers.

But now that it was actually looming up in front of me I was beginning to feel nervous. After all, I was not even fifty yet and it felt as if I was digging my own grave. Did I really want to become a retired, tweedy village colonel already? I loved living in the house with its idyllic garden, and both Caroline and I were greatly looking forward to spending some uninterrupted time with each other at last. But was this really going to be enough to keep me occupied? It all seemed so parochial, so inward-looking, so boring. I came back to the thought: if I was told I was dying next month, what have I achieved?

I needed to make a definite move now if I was going to change the direction of my life before it was too late. I was pretty sure that my career in the army was winding down; it seemed unlikely that I would be offered any more good jobs. I must start looking around outside for something more. I began writing to organizations like Oxfam and Save the Children to see if I could get into the field of helping with disaster relief in some way. I felt my training and personality would be well suited to this kind of work. I had no specialization, like engineering or medical training, but my experience of command at various levels would mean that I had something useful to offer. If there was an earthquake or flood somewhere, for instance, I imagined that they must need people who were able to get a grip on the situation and organize things. That was where I believed my strengths lay.

Caroline was not altogether surprised when I told her what I was thinking of doing. She had always accused me of being sentimental, easily moved to tears by puppies and small children with big eyes. She could see why I wanted to do it, but she was nervous. 'I know exactly what will happen,' she said one evening, only half joking, 'you'll go off to some Third World country to build a hospital and you'll get over-emotional and fall in love with the first pretty young nurse you meet.'

'Don't be ridiculous,' I laughed, anxious to allay any fears she might have.

The letters did provoke some responses and I was beginning to meet people and make contacts in the charity world when my boss, Lieutenant General Sir Richard Swinburn, called me into his office.

'You've been posted, Mark.' He watched my reactions carefully. 'Where do you think you are going?'

There then followed a guessing game as he steered me round the world with hints like 'east a bit' and 'west a bit', during which I displayed an embarrassing lack of geography, until we ended up in Croatia. Like most people in England at the time, I had been following events in Yugoslavia. I had watched scenes of civil war on the television news as the country split up into different ethnic factions. I knew that the Serbs and the Croats had been fighting over Croatia ever since it had declared independence, and that the Serbs had started to capture territory, with a great deal of destruction and bloodshed. Beyond that I knew little about the country or its people.

'That's marvellous!' I enthused, and he looked rather surprised.

'You're pleased?'

'Oh, absolutely,' I assured him. 'Any opportunity to get out and command something again.' What I really wanted to say was, 'Anything to get out of this place,' but I managed to check myself.

Here was my chance to escape from my desk and do something positive in an area where I knew that terrible things were happening, and to be involved in the making of modern history again. It meant that I could postpone thinking about what to do with the rest of my life and concentrate on the next few months. Although the outside world still had no idea of just how shocking the atrocities being committed in the name of ethnic cleansing were, it was becoming clear that the situation was worsening quickly and something had to be done if the whole area was not to dissolve into a war which might then spread to the rest of Europe, just as it had in 1914.

Now that I knew I would be out there within three months, I started to take a more active interest in the news as it reached us through the media. My appointment was to be Commander of the British Contingent (COMBRITCON) of the United Nations Protection Force (UNPROFOR). I soon realized that it was not likely to be the most onerous of jobs as the contingent was very small, but that did not worry me.

Just getting back into active service was enough. It was a great relief.

It was to be a six-month unaccompanied tour from June to December, which meant that I would not have to uproot Caroline again and she could continue to settle into village life. Because we had talked about my frustrations with the job at Aldershot, she was not surprised when I came home fired with enthusiasm about this new offer. For her, the army had also added the carrot that after this job in Croatia they would try to find me a job at Wilton, close to home. She was quite used to me going off for months at a time, and the prospect of my coming back to a job down the road which would allow us finally to settle down to a life together in Wiltshire made her less unhappy about me going away once more. I chose not to think about how I would feel once I had returned to England again. I was just grateful to have been given this reprieve before I had to make any final decisions about changing the course of my life.

The force I was to take over had been out in Croatia for six weeks by the time I arrived at the end of June. I had attended a great many briefings to fill in the large gaps in my knowledge about the area and its complex problems, but I was still not prepared for the sights and tales that I would see and hear when I got out there.

By chance I bumped into a friend of mine, Brigadier Jeremy Phipps, and told him that I had been posted to Croatia. 'That's fascinating,' he said, his face lighting up, 'you must meet my stepfather.'

'Why?'

'Well, he knows a bit about Yugoslavia. His name's Fitzroy Maclean.'

I was surprised to discover this connection. Sir Fitzroy Maclean was a young SAS officer in the Second World War, when Yugoslavia was invaded and occupied by the Germans. The Serbs and Croats were then fighting each other at the same time as fighting the Germans. Winston Churchill pulled

Maclean out of the desert, where he was serving at the time, and asked him to go to Yugoslavia to find out which of the local armies – the 'Partisans' or the 'Chetniks' as they were called then – was most effective at killing Germans, and to give that army whatever support it needed to set up an effective resistance movement. So Maclean was parachuted into Yugoslavia, met up with Tito, who was in charge of the Partisans, and decided that the Croats were the ones to back. There has been controversy since, some people saying that he backed the wrong force, but he made his decision and it changed the course of history for the area, leading to Tito's long and highly successful rule after the war.

Maclean spent three years of the war getting supplies to the Partisans to help them in their struggle against the Germans. It was a highly effective resistance movement because of the nature of the countryside, which is one of the problems that face the peace-keeping forces in the area today. The mountains, forests and valleys are perfect terrorist country, ideal for staging ambushes, blocking roads and blowing up bridges. Sir Fitzroy Maclean was consequently a legend in the area and I was very keen to meet him.

Jeremy rang his stepfather and he invited Caroline and me up to his house on the west coast of Scotland for dinner and an overnight stay. We drove up and arrived at an enormous, beautiful mansion on the banks of a loch, where Sir Fitzroy and Lady Maclean live in peaceful splendour.

'We're going out to dinner this evening,' Sir Fitzroy told me during the course of the afternoon, 'and I've invited another chap and his wife to meet you. He's called Mladen Grbin. He's a Croatian, born and bred on the island of Korčula, where we have a house, by the way. You and your wife must go and stay there when you have some time off. He is naturalized British now, married to a British girl, Carol, and lives in Glasgow.'

I felt rather ignorant at dinner, never having been to Yugoslavia, but it was very interesting trying to absorb some of the atmosphere as they talked about a country which was a first home to Mladen and a second one to his wife and to the Macleans.

At the end of the evening, as we were saying goodbye to the Grbins, Mladen shook me firmly by the hand. 'Do keep in touch when you go out there,' he said. Although I did not know it at the time, meeting those two men was to be my first lucky break, and both would help me enormously in the tasks which lay ahead. At the time it just seemed like a nice start to the mission, giving me some valuable background impressions from some highly knowledgeable and perceptive people.

3

The Shock of Destruction

The first surprise was to discover that Croatia is only two hours' flying time from Britain. I had imagined that it would be at least four hours. The realization that there was an active war zone that close to London, Paris, Vienna and other supposedly safe and stable European capitals was a shock. Yugoslavia had shared borders with Austria, Italy and Greece, all places we think of as peaceful and secure. Now the world was confused by the new names which kept appearing in the media: Croatia, Bosnia, Serbia. How did all these places fit together? I had no more idea than the next man.

I was also surprised by how seemingly untouched and civilized Zagreb was, just another city going about its business, albeit with more than its fair share of uniformed troops, civilian police and white UN and other aid vehicles in evidence. Everything was working as normal – shops, hotels, transport. On the descent in the plane I had seen no signs of the burning villages and mass destruction which I had watched on television before leaving England. The city was untouched, still full of attractive buildings; operas were being performed as normal, restaurants and bars were buzzing with conversation, and life was continuing as before.

I was met at Zagreb airport by Colonel Christopher Price, from whom I was taking over. My new home was to be Pleso Camp, next to the airport, which had been an old Yugoslav Airforce base. At that stage there were 1,000 UN troops in the camp, which was to be the logistics base for all the UN operations in Croatia, but by the time I became Camp Commandant a few months later that number had doubled.

The Yugoslav Airforce, which by then had become the Serbian Airforce, had done as much damage as possible to the fabric of the camp before departing for Serbia, leaving taps running so that water got everywhere, and breaking things up.

At the beginning of the Serbo-Croat war the Serbs had been besieged in the camp by the Croats and had laid mines all round the perimeter, many of which were still there. 'Be careful not to go anywhere which doesn't have a hard surface at the moment,' Christopher warned me. 'We still have a lot of clearing to do and several people have been blown up. It'll be a long time before we have made the whole area completely safe.'

My job as COMBRITCON was to command a force of 250 people, mainly medical, including the 24th Field Ambulance, commanded by a woman, Lieutenant-Colonel Lois Lodge, plus some signals, engineers, transport personnel and cooks. It was a self-contained little force whose role was to provide the second-line medical support for UNPROFOR in Croatia. This meant we had responsibility for transporting any injured or sick soldiers from the regimental aid posts at their places of duty to the hospital in Zagreb. So we were basically providing an ambulance service throughout Croatia, from Vukovar in the east to Knin in the south, a distance of about 700 kilometres.

The ambulances we were provided with had been used in the Gulf War and were completely clapped out. We never knew for sure if they would make it back whenever they went out to collect wounded, and it did not take long for the new standing joke in UNPROFOR to be: 'What goes into a Protected Area but can't get out? A British Army Ambulance.' It was not an auspicious start to our assignment.

For the majority of the men in the contingent it was a frustrating job which entailed a lot of waiting around for something to happen to anyone in the UN. The greatest threat was from unexploded mines. We were not there to look after the local people as their own medical services were still just functioning.

Soldiers are generally happy with their lot and do not mind living rough – which most of us were – if they are kept busy and feel they are doing a worthwhile job. Boredom on a six-month operational term away from home and family can be dangerous, quickly eroding morale. It says much for the commanders of this small British contingent, dotted around the country, that they managed to keep their men motivated and well disciplined.

Under the Vance Plan – the peace agreement brokered between the Serbian and Croatian governments by Cyrus Vance, at that time the UN Special Mediator – these UN Protection Forces were spread all over Croatia in four UN protected areas. The eastern sector around Vukovar had been captured and held by Serbs. The western sector was based in Daruvar and was divided in half, with the Serbs occupying the southern part, which they had captured from the Croats. The village of Lipik, a place I had yet to discover but which was going to change my life, was right on the dividing line. The north and south sectors ran along the Dalmatian coast. In all these areas the Serbs had attacked and captured land from the Croatians. Under the Vance Plan the Serbian and Croatian governments had agreed to allow the UN forces in after the fighting had stopped. The two armies would then withdraw to designated, agreed lines (5 kilometres from the ceasefire line for infantry, 10 kilometres for tanks and armoured personnel carriers, and 15 kilometres for artillery). All this I had had explained to me at briefings before I left the UK. In the protected areas the UN forces were acting like militarized police forces, keeping the two sides apart whilst encouraging the people to rebuild their shattered lives. In reality, UNPROFOR was protecting the Serbs in areas totalling about one-third of Croatia, which they had seized. It was not surprising, therefore, that the majority of Croats had little time for the UN, and we often heard 'UNPROFOR go home' shouted at us as we passed.

On my first day, while Christopher was still showing me round the local area, we heard that plans were being made to fly aid into Sarajevo, down in Bosnia. The city was just coming to the notice of the world as the latest major trouble spot in the area. It had come under siege from the Serbs, who had penned in the Muslims and were now shelling the city from the hills. President Mitterrand had made a daring and dangerous flight into the city, to show that it could be done and to galvanize international governments into action. The RAF sent a Hercules plane to be part of this new initiative, and organizing this took up most of the time during my handover period from Christopher. The young crew of the Hercules were specialists in dangerous flying. They gave the impression of being rather undisciplined cowboys, but quickly proved themselves to be highly professional. I had always been a very traditional soldier, comfortable when toeing the line and conforming to the expectations of my colleagues and superiors, and I had often been shocked – and rather impressed – by people like these pilots, and certain SAS officers, who are so confident of their abilities that they do not worry about flaunting their individuality.

The following day Christopher suggested we went in his Land-Rover to Sector West, which was the closest to Zagreb, so that I could get a feel for what had been going on over the last year. We headed out on to the main Belgrade Highway. To start with, the only unusual feature was the lack of traffic on this major European trunk road, which made the trip eerie. The houses and fields on the sides of the road looked untouched by war, with the small farmers going about their daily business of feeding their families and trying to create enough of a surplus to supply some of their friends and neighbours.

We came off the motorway into Okućani, a village which the Serbs had captured and were still holding. The buildings had been badly damaged in the fighting and there were still several tanks and other weapons lying discarded around the ruins. Christopher was obviously used to these sights, but I was not prepared for the horror I would experience at the devastation which I saw all around me. Suddenly we had moved from a peaceful farming area into a war zone where there had been terrible destruction. I didn't know what to think. I was in a state of shock as we drove on up to Daruvar and down to Pakrac and Lipik. All these areas had suffered heavy fighting in the war between August and December the previous year, and all that was left was ruins.

'This,' Christopher gestured at the endless rows of burnt-out, roofless houses in Lipik, 'is the result of ethnic cleansing. The Serbs captured the town first and destroyed all the houses and buildings owned by Croats. Then the Croats retook the town and destroyed all the buildings owned by Serbs.' The result was that every single building had been blown up and burnt out. Every roof was gone, every window was a gaping hole, many rimmed with fang-like glass fragments. Floors, walls, everything inside the houses lay in piles of rubble. This was the effect of hatred so strong that people were willing to destroy the homes of their former friends and neighbours rather than leave them in a habitable state for their enemies to return to. Soldiers had broken into ordinary people's family homes with the sole intention of destroying them and killing anyone they found inside. The human corpses had been removed many months before but the rotting remains of their homes could not disappear so easily. In some cases houses had been sliced in half, revealing the insides of rooms with old furniture, bedding and clothing still in place. Anything usable had been looted.

'This isn't like being attacked by a professional army,' Christopher went on as I stared around in silent horror. 'A real army would keep captured amenities like hospitals intact so that they could use them, but these people have wrecked everything. They have even smashed up the public swimming pool. The point is that if you drive someone out of their home town they are going to want to get back to their homes, and will continue to plot and fight to do so. But if you destroy the town, so that there is nothing to come back to, they might as well move off and start their lives again somewhere else. It is a crazy philosophy which results in everyone losing everything.'

Indirect shelling from the surrounding hills and direct tank fire had also helped to raze many of the buildings to the ground, pounding and pummelling them until they were reduced to piles of broken masonry with splintered beams and twisted metal sticking out at angles, like bones from smashed bodies. Roads were riddled with potholes and trees and parkland had been destroyed.

These villages were ghost towns: all the people had been killed or chased away. Occasionally we would pass a house where someone, usually an old man or woman, had managed to find shelter by boarding up one room or a garage, and was trying to eke out a nervous, mournful existence in the ruins of their former life. The occasional mongrel dog or chicken could be seen scratching around in the rubble for anything edible, but these few sad figures only served to highlight the silence and emptiness of the streets and houses.

I had seen images of these scenes on television, but the small screen can never show the extent of the damage caused in campaigns like this. It was not until I was driving through the area, travelling along miles of road where every single building we passed was a ruin, that I realized the depth of the destruction and felt the full impact of what the people must have gone through in those months. I had had limited experiences of insurrections and campaigns of terror and bombing in places like Borneo, Cyprus and Belize, but I had never seen anything like this. I remained in stunned silence all the way back to Pleso Camp as I tried to take in the enormity of what I had seen. I don't think Christopher realized just how profoundly shaken I had been.

When Christopher flew out a few days later I felt a sudden surge of panic at being left in charge of a situation where I still felt that I hardly understood anything of what had happened. I needed to find out as much as possible as soon as possible, and I decided to go down to Sarajevo to see what it was like and to visit a doctor of ours, Major Vanessa Lloyd-Davies, who was responsible, along with a couple of corporals, for providing the medical support for the UN headquarters down there. The headquarters was located in the old Post Office building, which had been converted for the purpose.

The hills surrounding the city were bristling with Serbian guns which had the capability to fire on planes coming in and out. The soldiers manning the weapons were not under military control as we understand it, and were quite likely, had they imbibed enough slivovic, the fiery local plum brandy, to decide to take pot shots at anything which went past looking like a fat pigeon. I was very aware of this as our Hercules droned down into Bosnia, and felt an exhilarating mixture of fear and excitement.

The RAF crews quickly adopted a landing technique called the 'Khe Sanh Landing', which the Americans had invented in Vietnam. It involved flying in very high until they were over the airfield. Then they would put the nose down and head almost vertically for the ground, hopefully pulling out at the last minute and landing horizontally. This way they offered themselves as targets for the shortest possible time. It made for an extremely exciting ride for the passengers. On the way out, when they were not carrying any cargo, they would reverse the process by getting up maximum speed, flying low over the length of the runway before firing upwards like corks from champagne bottles, which provided another exhilarating sensation.

The Commander of the UN Forces, a very suave Indian general called Satish Nambia, was flying in on another plane at the same time and was going to be giving a press conference. Martin Bell from BBC News and Michael Nicholson from

ITN flew in on the same plane as me. Strangely enough, I had connections with both reporters. I had been to school with Martin at the Leys in Cambridge. He was a little older than me and would not have remembered me, but I recalled that he was a good swimmer. I had also met Michael Nicholson on a family skiing holiday many years before. We had made friends with him and his wife Diana and their two sons, who were the same age as ours. They had taken their boys with them whilst we had not, and both families thought the other had made the right decision. Michael and I both remembered this, but we had no idea how much impact our next meeting in Sarajevo was going to have on our lives later on, and on Martin's life too.

The landing worked and we arrived safely on the tarmac. As we got out of the plane bullets whistled over our heads. I quickly ducked down but soon noticed that I was the only one to do so; everyone else, including Martin and Michael, who were both old hands at living in war zones, seemed to be taking virtually no notice, walking casually over to the airport buildings. I soon came to realize that veteran news reporters actually see far more action than any modern soldier, always making their way to where the fighting is fiercest and often arriving long before any peace-keeping forces have been assembled.

There was complete confusion in the city at the time. The Serbs were firing at the Muslims, and the Muslims were firing back at them. Different areas of the city were held by different factions and both sides were prone to fire at the UN forces from time to time and then deny they had anything to do with it, passing the blame on to the other side. It was almost impossible to tell where most of the shells and rounds of gunfire were actually coming from.

Vanessa Lloyd-Davies, a dynamic English country lady, was extremely worried that she had not got enough medical supplies should the fighting in Sarajevo escalate and UN troops become the target or get caught in the cross-fire. As soon as I arrived, she grabbed me to show me just how little she had in the case of an emergency, telling me exactly what she needed so that she could set up an effective hospital in the car park under the hastily converted Post Office.

'If we take a direct hit on this building,' she explained, 'we could have thirty or forty people badly injured, maybe more. I simply don't have the supplies or equipment to deal with a situation like that. It would be a disaster.' I had to agree with her. She is an immensely brave woman and I was delighted when, later on, she received an MBE for gallantry, along with one of her men, Sergeant Newitt. During one action they displayed particular courage when some mortar bombs landed on a group of children playing in the street outside UN Headquarters. After the first round fell, blowing many of the children to pieces, they ran out to pick up the survivors while more bombs were raining down on them.

Vanessa then asked me to talk to General Lewis MacKenzie, the Canadian who was in charge at the time, to support her cause. What she said seemed to me to make perfect sense and I was happy to act as her champion. She gave me a list of vital supplies and I went to see the general. It was by then late into the night, but I found him still working in his office. I put Vanessa's case for her and he agreed with us.

'Go for it,' he said, so I started sending signals back and forth to England. The supplies arrived amazingly quickly. A number of people were upset that I had waded in and taken action without due bureaucratic consultation, but the arguments eventually died down, drowned out by the noise of everything going on around. That night I stayed in Sarajevo, using one of the many camp beds which had been set up at the headquarters, and fell asleep to the noise of continuous gunfire.

I went down to Sarajevo several times in the following months and saw how the city was being systematically destroyed. There was permanent shelling and shooting, with tracer bullets streaking across the sky at night. In all the times I went there I think there was only one occasion when I wasn't actually fired at by someone, either directly or indirectly. There was so much lead flying around that it was certainly the most dangerous place I had ever been called upon to work in.

Before leaving England I had met my Commander in Chief, General Sir John Waters, who was commanding the United Kingdom Land Forces. 'I'm coming out to see you in two weeks' time,' he told me. 'I'll be interested to hear what you think of the situation.' He is a man who has a reputation for asking very pertinent and tricky questions of his officers. I therefore knew that I needed to make sure I understood the situation before he arrived, so that I could brief him authoritatively. I would have to get round Croatia very quickly and visit all the units in all the areas if I was going to be in any position to give him my impressions.

After the return from Sarajevo to Zagreb I set out in my Land-Rover, with a marvellous Scottish driver called Lance-Corporal Anderson. It was a very slow and rather uncomfortable vehicle which seemed to take forever to get anywhere, leaving us both feeling drained and hot at every destination. We headed south to Knin, visiting Sector North on the way, then over to Vukovar in Sector East to see our people there. I spent the night in a small hotel in a nearby village on the edge of the Danube, which I soon realized was any colour but blue, and read Fitzroy Maclean's wonderful book, *Eastern Approaches*, which describes what happened in the area during the Second World War.

The following morning when I went to pay my bill there was a shy teenage girl on the desk. When she realized I was English and her boss was not listening, she started to talk to me quietly. She was Serbian and had lived all her life with her family in a nearby town called Osijek. When the war started and the Serbs attacked Vukovar and the surrounding area, she had to leave with her family for their safety. Her father said he would come back later when he had arranged his business affairs and they had never heard from him again. Confidentially she told me that she thought the Serbs, her own people, were wrong in their actions, and she was deeply saddened that her life as a student in Osijek had been ruined and she would never see her Croatian and Muslim friends again. I heard similar views from other Serb students in all areas where the Serbs had ejected Croatians and Muslims, and it gave me a glimmer of hope for the future that they, the younger generation, realized the madness and wickedness of their elders.

On a later trip to Vukovar, travelling along the Belgrade highway, I was reading a particularly good book while my driver put his foot down. He suddenly ducked down and there was a crump! crump! on the side of the road as a couple of rounds of artillery landed. We drove on to Vukovar to find some soldiers of mine there who had driven along the same road half an hour earlier. 'You'll never guess what happened to us on the way up here,' they said as we arrived. 'We were stopped by the Croatian army. They had a rocket launcher on the road. They fired some rockets into Serbia and then once they had done that they waved us on.'

'Show me on the map where that was,' I said.

When they pointed to the spot it was exactly where we had been, and I realized we had been on the receiving end of the return fire from the Serbs half an hour later!

On every road there were numerous UN roadblocks, all manned by different nationalities – Polish, Jordanian, Russian, Canadian, Nigerian. At each of them we had to stop and explain ourselves. On the way to Vukovar we pulled up at one which was manned by some Nepalese soldiers. As I had spent most of my service with Gurkhas I was delighted to see them. As Lance-Corporal Anderson drew up he watched open-mouthed as I sprang out and began talking away to them in Nepali.

We compared the relative merits of different curries as we

bumped on along the cratered roads to our next destination. Vukovar had been flattened with artillery and tank fire from the Serbs and looked like Dresden in the Second World War. No one could estimate how many people had been killed in the carnage.

From Vukovar we headed for Daruvar, where the headquarters of Sector West was located. On the way back through the sector Corporal Anderson casually remarked that there was a Nepalese unit based in the village of Lipik.

'That's on the way, isn't it?' I asked.

'Yes, sir.'

'Well, let's drop in on them. Maybe they'll give us a curry.'

'Yes, sir.'

Deciding to go for that curry was probably the most fateful decision I have ever made. From that moment everything was going to change. My life was going to be turned upside down, as were the lives of my wife and children. If Corporal Anderson had not mentioned that Nepalese company, none of the following story would have happened, and my life would probably have continued on the course I had taken for granted since, as a teenager, I had decided to go into the army. It was 10 July and we were approaching the hottest part of the year.

4

The Fateful Curry

Lipik was once an elegant spa town, visited by the wealthy and aristocratic classes of Europe for its curative mineral waters. At the centre of the town were a hospital and baths, beside which had stood a Victorian concert hall and esplanade of shops and cafés built around formal public gardens. It had been a place of great beauty, but now it was a wasteland, with only haunting reminders of its past in the few bits of broken statuary and the shattered arches and twisted trellis-work of the ruined Kursalon concert hall, lit by the hot afternoon sun.

The Nepalese company was based in part of the windowless, shrapnel-scarred hospital which they had managed to patch up enough to make safe. Because it was midsummer, glass in the windows was not needed. Corporal Anderson drove us into the gardens, along an avenue of once beautiful trees which had now had their tops knocked off by shells but still retained some of their original regimented style. We came to a halt at the guard point, and I climbed out and started talking to the soldiers in their language. The hot afternoon air was full of exotic smells, some from the remains of the gardens surrounding us and some from the kitchen which was catering for the soldiers.

The role of these UN detachments in such towns was to patrol and keep the peace, helping to get things back to normal, arranging the restoration of telephones, electricity and water supplies wherever possible, and offering protection to such of the population as was left or tried to return. In Lipik, right on the front line between the Serbs and the Croats, their job was also to stop the two sides from having

33

another go at each other and to help them get their once thriving town going again.

The soldiers were surprised and delighted to meet someone who spoke Nepali and were laughing and joking when their company commander, Major Devi Limbu, who had been sitting on a balcony above the guard post, stood up to see what was happening.

'Hallo,' he called down. 'Who are you?' I introduced myself. 'Come up,' he beckoned me.

I walked up the stairs inside the building and came out on to the verandah where he was sitting. He was with about four other Nepalese officers and a young woman in a white doctor's coat.

'Colonel Cook,' Major Limbu shook my hand, 'may I introduce you to the local doctor, Dr Topić?' I shook her hand, reading the badge which she had pinned to her lapel saying 'Dr M. Topić', to make sure I memorized the name out of politeness. I could see immediately that she was an exceptionally vivacious young woman, a very unusual person to meet in a place where most of the young people had fled or been killed and where not many people had anything left to smile about. 'Will you join us for coffee, Colonel Sahib?' Major Limbu indicated a chair and I sat down. Coffee was produced and we talked, explaining what we were all doing there. The young doctor was the first Croatian I had been able to communicate with properly since arriving in the country, due to the language barrier. I had a million questions I wanted to ask about how it actually felt to see your country being destroyed around you, and how people found the strength to go on with their lives.

'Before the war I was a doctor here in Lipik,' she explained in rather halting English, compensating for her limited vocabulary with a lot of theatrical gestures. 'Now I spend alternate weeks here and in Zagreb, sharing with another doctor so that there is always someone here for the people to come to. It is very hard to live in Lipik all the time at the moment. There is nothing left, really, we have to build everything again from the start.' While she was in Lipik, she explained, she lived in a room at the hospital and tended the sick who were left in the town; when in Zagreb she stayed at her aunt's flat.

'Would you stay and join us for a curry, Sahib?' Major Limbu asked, just as I had hoped he would. I didn't need to be asked twice.

'Well,' he said, 'I would like to make a suggestion. I have one or two things to do. So, while the supper is being cooked, perhaps Dr Topić might like to show you round the hospital grounds, so that you can see for yourself the extent of the damage which has been done.'

'Of course.' The doctor beamed at me and the smile lit her whole face. 'I would be pleased to.'

We went downstairs, followed by a couple of Nepalis and Corporal Anderson. The light was just beginning to fade as we strolled off into the shattered grounds, and I tried to imagine how wonderful it must have looked just a few months before. We walked along a path between two-foot-high privet hedges that ran along the edges of the lawns, which were covered in debris and cratered by shells. Seen from the air, these lawns would have formed a precise geometrical pattern. All the paths and miniature hedges led to the Fontana, a fountain which had once been the centrepiece of the gardens. We were now directly in front of what had obviously once been a wonderfully graceful façade, but which was now pockmarked by shrapnel.

'This,' the doctor explained, 'is the Kursalon. The pride of Lipik. Here there was a concert hall, dance floors, restaurants. It was a famous building in the area. You can see,' she gestured at the broken arches and the rubble which had crashed down on to the tiled floors, 'it was very beautiful.'

I looked back across the gardens towards the hospital. Elegant street lamps, designed like candelabras, stood unlit and rusting amid the twisted and broken park benches. From this angle I could see more clearly how the avenues of trees

must have looked before the shells started to fall among
them. Around the sides of the park were rows of once elegant mansions, now all destroyed. I turned back to the
Kursalon's jagged ruins, my eyes drawn to a solitary cherub
which had somehow escaped the bullets and now gestured
sadly with an outstretched arm at all the devastation around
it.

As we walked on, Dr Topić talked about how the town
had been before the war, how the Fontana and the Kursalon
had been the symbols of Lipik and how their destruction had
affected the people.

'Lipik is the only town in this whole war which has been
captured twice, once by each side.' She shrugged, unable to
hide her anger at what had happened. 'And so it was destroyed twice, and again by the shells from the hills over
there.' She gestured to distant mountains, territory which was
still held by Serbs even though the guns had temporarily
fallen silent. 'The farmland between here and the mountains
used to belong to the people here. They can see it from what
is left of their homes, but now it is in Serbian territory. They
can't go out there because the soldiers are still watching and
the guns are still pointing.' She held me spellbound as I tried
to imagine how a girl who had witnessed so much suffering
could remain so vivacious.

'You know,' she went on, 'if it had not been for the thirty-
five men who volunteered to stay and fight, the Serbs would
have marched down here much earlier. We would never have
been able to get them out, and this would now be part of
Serbian-held territory. You and your army would be protecting the Serbs here instead of us, like you are protecting them
in other parts of our country.' Her voice sounded as if she was
teasing me, but in her eyes I could see a real anger flaring.
'So, these people who have come back to the town have to
look out on to fields that they used to own and farm, which
are now behind enemy lines, and they are prevented from
taking that land back by you and your UN forces. Everyone

is protected, but no one is left with anything worth protecting.'

'What happened to the thirty-five men?' I wanted to know.

'The Serbs never knew how many of them there were. They thought there was a much bigger force down here. They had no way of telling. They could have just walked in if they had wanted. How could a few men with hunting rifles stop tanks and trained soldiers? The first man who commanded the resistance was killed, so they replaced him with another, he was killed, and the next one, and the next one. These were all men from the village. Friends of mine. Nearly everyone you meet here now has been shot or wounded somehow. All of them have lost their homes and some of their families.'

Behind the Kursalon had been a modern hotel for people who came to convalesce and take the waters, but now it was a burnt-out shell. Beyond that were several acres of woods, complete with a wrought-iron bandstand on a hill, but the trees which had been felled by the shells lay tangled on the ground, covered in weeds which no one had yet had the energy to clear.

'Oh, listen.' I stood still, unable to believe that I was actually hearing so many nightingales singing in one place, a place where until recently the only audible noise had been the rumble of tanks, the thump of artillery and the crack of snipers' guns. 'Isn't that wonderful? We hardly ever hear them in England any more.'

'Come on,' she beckoned me. 'I will show you the swimming-pool area. It was once very beautiful, one of the best in the area, and now . . . well, you will see.'

She started off into the wood and Christopher Price's warning about mines came back to me. 'Are you sure?' I called out after her. 'Has this area been cleared of mines?'

She turned and laughed at me as I dithered on the edge of the tangled undergrowth. 'Come on, Colonel, I will look after you. I walk here every day, I know it is safe, just follow me.'

This was going against all my military training, which had taught me never to walk in areas like this until the sappers had been through. I also knew that a number of UN personnel had been blown up on mines in previous weeks. Thousands of shells had landed in the park in the last year, crashing through the tops of the trees and landing God only knew where. But my pride would not allow me to hang back while this brave young woman showed me up. I took a deep breath and shuffled cautiously after her, peering nervously into the undergrowth before each footstep while she strode ahead, jumping over fallen branches and pushing aside shrubbery while I pussyfooted along behind her.

Eventually my military instincts prevailed. 'I really don't think we should be doing this,' I said as firmly as I could, aware that Corporal Anderson and the others were following behind us. 'Perhaps we should get back to the hospital.'

'Okay,' she turned and smiled mockingly, 'whatever you say. We will go this way, and I will show you the children's home instead. Perhaps I will show you the swimming pool another day.' With a sigh of relief I followed her down the path to some more ruined buildings. 'This,' she gestured at the tall shells of walls with their empty windows showing the collapsed ceilings and floors inside, 'is where the first shell of the war fell, on top of the orphans of Lipik.' She paused for a moment, biting into her lip as she remembered before resuming her breezy tone. 'The children were my patients. They used to come to me with their problems, especially the girls. Those cellars,' she pointed to some tiny windows at the bottom of one of the ruins, 'are where they lived for twenty days in all.'

'Where are they now, the children?'

'In Selce, in another home, down on the coast. I would like to visit them but it is a long way and it is hard to get there. I have spoken to them on the phone. They are in a building which was already full before they arrived. They want to come back to Lipik. That is what they all tell me. But there is nothing for them to come back to.'

'These children are Croatian?'

'They are a mixture, just as the whole of Lipik was,' she explained. 'Some are Croats, some are Serbs, some are Muslim, some are Romany, some are Czechoslovakian. They don't know any differences. They have no quarrel with one another. They believe they are all one family. There is one boy whose father was a Serb and was killed fighting close to here when the Croatian soldiers returned. They found the boy with his father's body and took him to the orphanage in Selce. He talks of Lipik as his home just like the others.'

'Were any of the children hurt?'

'No, it has been miraculous, they are all unharmed physically. But emotionally . . .' She shrugged. 'The only fatality was their dog. He wandered out of the cellar one day and did not return. I think they found some pieces of him later.'

'That's sad.'

'Not so sad.' She laughed. 'Bric was not a nice dog. Only one little boy, called Stanko, really loved him, and he bit Stanko.'

I gazed up at the walls, trying to imagine what it must have been like. 'All this damage was done by shelling?'

'No.' She shook her head. 'When the Serbs came down out of the hills, this became a front line. They blew what was left of this building up, just as they did all the houses. If the children had still been here they would have blown them up too, or worse. When the Croats came back and recaptured the town on 6 December there was more fighting in the streets, and more damage still to the buildings. This is all that remains.'

We stood for a few moments amidst the rubble, looking at the gloomy, gutted buildings with the sun setting behind them and the nightingales singing in the background. I was moved almost to tears.

'Perhaps,' I coughed to clear my throat, 'we should go back and see if the curry is ready yet.'

By the time we got back to the balcony the smell of the curry was wafting out into the grounds and Dr Topić held out her hand to say goodbye.

'Goodbye, Colonel Cook.' She smiled up into my face and I was aware of how very large, beautiful and brown her eyes were. 'I hope I will see you again some time.'

'Are you going to be in Zagreb next week?' I asked.

'Yes.' She nodded, watching me with the hint of a laugh. 'I will be.'

'Perhaps we could meet for a drink or something.' I had enjoyed her company and wanted more of it. I had never met anyone quite like her and I thought it would be fun to get away from Pleso Camp occasionally and mix with some locals. I wanted to understand more about someone who had been through so much and still managed to seem so dynamic. She appeared so very foreign and mysterious and different.

'That would be very nice. I would like that. This is my aunt's telephone number at the flat.' She wrote the number down and gave it to me. 'Goodbye.'

As she walked off I went upstairs to enjoy my supper with the major. Only later did I discover that she had been invited for curry before I turned up, and I was actually eating her meal.

As darkness descended, with the familiar sounds of the Nepalese soldiers all around and the delicious curry settling comfortably in my stomach, I was enjoying myself hugely, reminiscing about Nepal and the Gurkhas, when a mighty explosion filled the town, sending flocks of crows cawing into skies from the trees in the park and silencing all the other birds and insects. The soldiers scurried for their weapons and vehicles. What must have been one of the last houses standing in Lipik had been blown up.

Later that evening Corporal Anderson and I drove back to Zagreb, and the following day I was due to go back down to Sarajevo.

5

Consumed by the Fire

'Please,' Dr Topić said when I rang her a few days later, 'call me Marina.'

'Marina? I thought your name was Marica' (pronounced Maritza).

'To some people. But to my friends and family I am Marina.' She sounded rather breathless.

'Are you all right? Have I called at a bad moment?'

'No, I am sorry, I am just very surprised. I didn't think that I would hear from you. I thought that when you took my number you were just being polite, you know, a gentleman. I thought you would be very busy.'

'Well, I went down to Sarajevo yesterday, so I was busy then, but now I'm back in Zagreb and I wondered if you would like to meet for a drink or something this evening. Or do you already have an arrangement?'

'I can change it, it isn't a problem.'

'Wonderful. Where shall we meet?'

We arranged to meet at a restaurant and club in a lovely old building near the centre of town, close to the opera house. I already knew this place and she said she could easily find it. I was very keen to meet someone local and to get away from the army for a few hours. I was also keen to see her again. I got there first and she was not far behind. I was surprised by just how beautiful she was when she walked in. Before, she had been in her white coat, her face scrubbed of makeup, with her hair tied back. Now she was dressed up to go out in a big city and wearing makeup which accentuated her eyes even more. She looked stunning. I think I may have been rather taken aback. Her English was very heavily accented and I didn't speak a word of Croatian, so the small-talk got off to a rather slow start as we both laboured to tune in to the other's accent against the background noise of the bar. I started by asking a lot of very ignorant questions about her life in Croatia and I was beginning to feel rather awkward, wondering what I was doing there. But after a couple of drinks we both relaxed and the words began to flow more easily from both of us.

'So how long have you been going back to Lipik?' I asked conversationally.

'Just a few weeks. When the war started they set up a big medical centre in Pakrac, so that was where I went.' Her eyes seemed to glaze over slightly as she remembered her experiences there. 'They sent me over there for the day from Lipik because there were reports of many wounded from the street fighting, but I didn't manage to get out again for a month. It was a very bad time. The fighting was very heavy. There were many wounded. Sometimes I would go out to someone who had been shot and was too badly hurt to move. That made me a target like everyone else. Once I was trapped in a house for hours by gunmen. I was trying to get the wounded out to the medical centre. We saw so many terrible things.' She went quiet for a few moments, lost in a daydream. She sipped her drink and lit another cigarette, then gave a start as if I had taken her by surprise, interrupting her reverie. She smiled apologetically, gathered her thoughts and continued with her story.

'I joined the army and went to Vukovar just before it fell. The Serbs were bombarding it all the time. Very heavy shell-fire. All the time, Bang! bang! night and day. It drives people mad to begin with and then you stop hearing it. I was there for about two weeks, working all the time, trying to save as many lives as possible, but people were dying in such numbers. It was impossible. Then I came back to Pakrac again. I was the only doctor they had then. I was the only woman among about eight hundred men.'

It was obviously painful for her to talk about it. I didn't ask her anything else for a moment, letting her compose herself and enjoy her drink. After a few moments she continued.

'In October we started to get ready to retake Lipik from the Serbs and I looked after the soldiers in the army as it advanced. Many of my friends from that time were killed.' I could see tears forming in her eyes and she bit her lip to control herself.

'You don't have to talk about this if it is too painful.'

She looked at me for a few moments and then shook her head. 'No, it's okay. It's good to talk about it. Some of it. To get it out of my head a little. After we retook Lipik there was still fighting down the road in Pakrac because the Serbs had only moved back a little way. They continued to try to hold on to what they had gained. So I went back to the medical centre there to help.

'We were always frightened of capture. When we were evacuating some wounded Croatian soldiers in a truck, I sat beside the driver with a hand-grenade in my lap, ready to blow us all up if the Serbs intercepted us.

'It was all so confused, no one could really explain what was happening. When I was in the hospital one day, a UN officer came and asked for one of the patients by name. She was an old woman. I took him to her. He said, "I have good news for you: your son is safe and he has sent me to bring you to him, so you will be safe too." The woman looked at him blankly and said, "But I don't have a son." He checked her name and identity and insisted, "Your son has sent for you. He wants you to go to him." "But I have no son. If I did have a son he would not have gone into the mountains to join other men and fire shells on to a hospital where his mother was lying. He would not have caused his mother to go to hospital with his guns and the guns of his friends. I am a Serb. This doctor is a Croatian and she is taking better care of me than any son could have done." She refused to listen to him and he had to go. That is how confused everyone is. Families have been split and destroyed, sometimes turning on themselves. My brother is married to a woman who is a Muslim. One of her parents is Muslim and the other Croat. So whose side should they be on?'

She fell silent again and I decided to change the subject. 'So,' I said brightly, 'are you from Lipik originally?'

'No. I am Herzegovinian, from Mostar. That is where my family still are.'

'Oh, I'm sorry.' At that time the fighting in Mostar was very bad and it was hard to get news out of the city.

'Yes, it is hard. Sometimes I feel like I am an orphan and my parents are already lost to me.'

'What first brought you to Lipik?'

She looked up at me and her eyes were sad. 'I wanted to get away from an unhappy situation. I came to Lipik to work hard and I was able to make the children in the home into my children a little bit. It helped me with the pain I was suffering, but it didn't help me to forget.'

It seemed there was no subject you could bring up in this country without coming across some new and awful tragedy. I could see that this was a subject she did not want to talk about then. She was only thirty years old and already she had suffered more personal tragedy than most people endure in a lifetime. I was astonished by her courage and wanted desperately to hear more of her story, but I could see that I would have to wait for her to volunteer the information.

I made a more concentrated effort to lighten the conversation. 'I came to this restaurant the other day with one of my colleagues, Colonel Lois Lodge, that's how I knew about the place. We needed somewhere to entertain our Commander-in-Chief. We were told here might be suitable, so we came to book. So I'm coming back here in a few days for dinner.'

'Would you like to eat now?' she asked. 'Are you hungry? We could go and get a pizza if you like.'

'Yes, I would like that very much.'

A little later we were sitting in a pizza restaurant. 'So,' she smiled broadly, making the corners of her eyes crinkle mischievously, 'tell me about your boys.'

'Well, they are both in their teens, about to go to university, and I'm very proud of them. The elder one, Edward, is adopted. He thinks he might like to go into the army, which is rather a surprise to us, we didn't think he was interested in that sort of life. We conceived William very soon after Edward arrived.'

Our conversation rolled on along polite lines. We enjoyed the evening together and I knew I had to see her again. The glimpses which she had given me into her past had horrified me and I felt an overwhelming need to protect her from further hurt and help her to rebuild her life in any way I could.

A few days later I was back at the same restaurant, entertaining General Sir John Waters. A group of about fifteen of us accompanied the general and the bill was extortionate. The others were furious with me because I had chosen the place and done the ordering. When we got back to Pleso Camp there was nearly a mutiny. 'It might be all right on a colonel's pay,' my Chief of Staff grumbled, 'but the rest of us can't afford those sorts of prices.' I assured him that they were more than a colonel's pay could manage either, and promised to do my research more thoroughly next time.

The general was staying at a hotel in Zagreb during his visit, and he was being accompanied by his military assistant, Lieutenant-Colonel Peter Pearson, who happened to be a great friend of my family: Caroline is godmother to his son. I had known Peter for years. He had been my adjutant in the Gurkhas, virtually running the battalion for me. He is a very sparky, lively character, and he was an excellent foil for this very serious four-star general. We all travelled around together and the general began visibly to unwind in our company. Any formality finally evaporated on the second day of the visit when we drove down to Sector North and stopped in a burnt-out village on the way back, for a picnic. The food had been given to us at Pleso Camp before we left and it must have been the worst picnic ever prepared, even in the army. Each box contained some dry bread and cheese. You wouldn't have expected a dog to eat it, let alone a four-star general. It was embarrassing to start with, but in the end there was nothing we could do but laugh.

That afternoon we drove the general back to Zagreb, from where he was returning to England in his private plane, and I rang Marina to invite her out for another evening. I had found she was on my mind a lot of the time while we were driving around and I was impatient to see her again. We went for a drink and a pizza as before, and then she took me up into the beautiful old town, showing me St Mark's Church, which became 'my church' for the rest of the time that I was stationed in Croatia.

While General Waters was with us I told him that I felt somewhat under-employed in the job they had given me and asked if there might be any special missions I could perform while I was in the area.

'When we go to see General Nambia,' he said, 'I will volunteer your services.'

True to his word, during our discussions he said, 'We've got Colonel Cook here. He's very experienced, with thirty years' military service in the Gurkhas. He's not overstretched at the moment, so if there is anything you would like him to do, feel free to use him.'

General Nambia was grateful for the offer and seemed interested in this prospect, and I was pretty sure there must be a need for exciting cloak-and-dagger work around the area. About a week later I received a call from General Nambia's Chief of Staff, a very serious Danish brigadier. 'Colonel Cook,' he barked, 'we want to speak to you immediately.'

Brimming with expectation, I rushed over to his office.

'You volunteered to do whatever we needed,' the brigadier confirmed.

'Yes,' I said eagerly, 'that's right.'

'General Nambia wants you to be Camp Commandant of Pleso Camp.'

'No, no, you don't understand,' I said quickly, 'that's not what we had in mind.'

'Colonel Cook,' he growled, 'that is an order. You will take over as Camp Commandant from the French colonel as soon as possible.'

So that left me running this enormous logistic base camp of over a thousand people, which doubled in size in the following months. I was responsible for everything down to the efficient functioning of the laundry, the feeding facilities, the transport, mines, drains, sewers and camp security, exactly the sort of work I had hoped I had escaped from in England. To begin with I was doing this as a part-time job with no extra help, although I quickly managed to build up a complete headquarters of around a dozen full-time international UN staff.

The day after General Waters left, Douglas Hurd, the British Foreign Secretary, came to see us at Pleso. I was amazed at how much the soldiers appreciated his visit: they all wanted to talk to him and take photographs of the occasion. After he had gone I received a phone call from an old friend of mine, John MacKinlay, a very intelligent chap who had been in the 6th Gurkhas. We had been at staff college together and he had recently left the army. He was now on a fellowship to Brown University in America, studying international peace-keeping operations.

'I'm coming to Zagreb this weekend,' he explained, 'with a friend of mine, Peter Praxmarer. We want to find out a bit about UNPROFOR. We've got all the right permits and bits of paper from UN Headquarters in New York. Do you think you could help us out with a few introductions and a bit of a guided tour of the area?'

'I'd be absolutely delighted to,' I replied, looking forward to seeing him again.

Having known John for years, I knew that he would be easy to brief because of his military experience. He would immediately understand what I was saying. I was surprised, however, by his aristocratic Austrian friend Peter, a long-haired academic who looked to me rather like an anti-war protester from the 1960s. As soon as I had John on his own, I expressed my surprise.

'Don't worry, Mark,' John grinned, 'he's a good chap really. He knows an awful lot about the history of Croatia.' This was the second person I had met in the last few days who was completely different to anything I had encountered in the army. I still found it hard not to judge people by the standards of army appearances. It was a habit I was keen to break, but it was proving harder than I had expected. Perhaps I had already started the transformation into a genuine Colonel Blimp.

'The best thing we can do,' I said, after I had been briefing them for an hour or two, 'is take you out in a vehicle and show you some of the area. I suggest we go to a small town called Lipik. It shows the problems very graphically and it only takes just over an hour by road.'

On the way to Lipik we went through a UN checkpoint manned by Jordanian soldiers and John asked if he could take some pictures. The sergeant there said that he would have to get permission from his officer and suggested we had a cup of tea while we waited. The soldiers made a delicious pot of scented tea and chatted pleasantly.

'You are from England?' the sergeant said to John and me. 'We listen all the time to BBC World News.'

'That's interesting, why is that?'

'Because we believe what they tell us and the news is always changing, always fresh, the best way of keeping up with what is going on in the world.' Here was a Jordanian sergeant in Croatia listening to the BBC World Service. It was good to know that something British was still so well thought of by other nations.

Eventually the officer came and agreed to let John take his pictures, and we moved on to Lipik. Peter was completely horrified by what he saw. 'This is ghastly,' he kept exclaiming, 'this is terrible, it mustn't be allowed to happen. We must do something. What are we going to do? We must turn this hospital complex into a monument to peace. Let's make a university of peace here. Let's build something. Make something good come from all this bad.' His ideas for the hospital complex and grounds grew grander and grander as he walked about. I knew that his plans were impractical. It would take millions to restore the whole complex, and who would give money for a project like that on the front lines of a war zone, when the whole thing could be destroyed again at any moment? But his enthusiasm was inspiring and it did set me thinking.

That night I took them back to their hotel in Zagreb. 'Tomorrow,' I told them, 'I'll take you into Sector North, into Serbian-held territory. Buy some bread and cheese and fruit and we'll have a picnic lunch.'

Corporal Anderson drove us up to the Plitvice Lakes, one of the greatest beauty spots in Europe with a series of waterfalls, lakes and woods. I had visited there once before and I knew that the Croatians felt very bitter at the way the Serbs had taken one of their great natural assets from them. As we picnicked beside the lake, Peter produced one of the most famous of travel books, *Black Lamb and Grey Falcon* by Rebecca West, about her travels in the area during the 1920s. He read us bits about Plitvice as we sat in the sun eating our lunch and looking at the views. It was an emotive experience for all of us, made especially so because there was no one else there.

'There is someone I would like you to meet this evening,' I told them as we drove back. 'She is the doctor from Lipik and she has had a terrible war. She is very sensitive about the subject of the UN and about British politicians, both of whom she feels are not being helpful out here. She doesn't think either of them understands the situation properly, or is doing anything about it. Like most Croatians, she cannot understand why the UN haven't just thrown the Serbs off the Croats' land.'

I had been very surprised by the vehemence of Marina's views of the British, whom she believed to be a cold, hard-hearted and uncaring nation. Only later did I discover that this is a perception which was taught to children in schools throughout Eastern Europe under the old Communist system. Pictures of Englishmen always depicted them in top hats with umbrellas over their arms and severe expressions on their faces.

Being academics, both Peter and John are very provocative. They like nothing better than picking arguments, either with one another or with anyone else who happens to be around. I was frightened they would goad Marina just to see what her reactions would be. I had seen enough of her to know that she held too many strong opinions to be willing to keep quiet if angered, and that her grasp of English was nowhere near strong enough to be able to spot irony in their voices.

'Please,' I begged them, 'whatever you do, don't upset her. She has suffered badly in the war, both mentally and physi-cally. I will never forgive you if you upset her and she walks out on us.' I realized that I felt intensely protective of Marina.

We arranged to meet at our usual club, but when the three of us got there it was closed because it was Sunday. We sat down on a bench opposite the entrance to wait for Marina.

'So, what does she look like?' John asked, scanning the street for likely candidates.

'I don't know.' I was puzzled to discover that I wasn't sure. 'I know she's very pretty. I suppose her hair is dark.' They both looked at me suspiciously, unable to believe that anyone could be so unperceptive as to meet someone three times and not be able to describe them.

When I spotted her I walked across the grass to greet her. 'Don't do that,' she ticked me off.

'Don't do what?' I was taken aback, unused to being admonished by anyone other than senior army officers.

'Don't cut across the grass, walk round the paths.'

'Oh.' I smiled meekly.

We went to find something to eat and had a very good evening. Peter knew so much about Croatian history that he was able to talk to Marina in depth. She was interested and he was gentle with her, as I had requested. During dinner a small boy arrived in the restaurant with a basket of red roses, wrapped individually as romantic gifts for ladies.

'Here,' Peter beckoned him over, 'I will have them all.' He scooped out the entire contents of the basket and handed them to a startled but pleased Marina. As we walked back to the car, we passed an old woman begging in the street. Peter reached into his pocket and pulled out all the money he had, handing it to the surprised and grateful lady. Such, I learned, was his generosity and kindness.

Marina was returning to Lipik on Monday and we arranged to meet her there in the afternoon so that she could show John and Peter around the town herself. By this time a few hundred people had come back to Lipik and were trying to rebuild their lives amongst the ruins of their homes. Marina was still running her surgery from the shell of the hospital. We spent the afternoon looking round with her before John left for America and Peter for Vienna.

I drove Peter to Zagreb railway station, where we went into a huge, drab, open bar to wait. It was like a scene from one of those great Russian novels, with crowds of soldiers in uniform coming and going to war. The train for Vienna was due at midnight. As it drew in he turned to say goodbye and handed me the Rebecca West book that we had been reading as a gift. He then embraced me and kissed me warmly on both cheeks in a European manner which took me completely by surprise.

This was only the second time in my life that I had been kissed by a man, something that doesn't happen to Englishmen very often. The first time was in Hong Kong when I had sent one of my Gurkha soldiers off on an adventure training course expedition on a yacht. The boat was hit and sunk by a typhoon 150 miles out in the South China Sea. The crew had been rescued in the middle of the night by a Royal Navy boat and brought back to Hong Kong, where I was waiting on the jetty, along with a crowd of the friends and relatives of the other seven survivors. This little Gurkha was the only one who had no wife or family to meet him. I felt sorry for him. 'It's all right for you lot,' I said, 'you've all got someone to greet you, what about this poor chap?' From somewhere a voice said, 'Give Sahib a kiss.' The poor little Gurkha was so relieved to get his feet on to dry land after this terrifying ordeal that he threw his arms around me and hung on for dear life.

For the next few days, after John and Peter left, I was busy with visits and another trip down to Sarajevo. At the end of the week I received a letter from John MacKinlay in America, thanking me for all my help. At the end he wrote: 'Continue to enjoy Lipik, but be careful not to be consumed by the fire that burns within Marina, that beautiful but troubled young doctor.'

For a few seconds I was shocked and puzzled that he should write such a thing. But I knew that John was an exceptionally perceptive man and anything he said was worth pondering on. Then I realized that his warning had come too late: I was already being consumed.

6

The Promise

I had so much to learn about the people I was supposedly there to help. I had no real understanding of how it felt to have been robbed of everything, to have had your family and friends raped or killed, your home and place of work destroyed and your lands seized, to be in continual fear for your life. I could not imagine what it felt like to be forced to accept the charity of other nations just to survive another week, with no way of taking charge of your own destiny again.

News reports from Sarajevo were being dispatched all over the world by then. Aid was coming in from everywhere to enable the people to survive until the siege could be lifted and normal life resumed. The following weekend I went down to Sarajevo again to see how our medics were getting on. Like many others, I rather enjoyed my trips down there, particularly the flights, as I normally went into the flight deck for take-off and landing. A lady from the Foreign Office in London used to fly out regularly, often at weekends, and we all reckoned she was a Sarajevo junkie. With so much going on, Sarajevo was certainly a very exciting place for a professional soldier to be. It always made the adrenalin flow a little faster.

During this particular visit I decided to go out with a UNHCR convoy, escorted by Canadian soldiers in armoured personnel carriers, to see how the aid was distributed. We came under sporadic fire as we lumbered our way through the Muslim-held territory on what should have been a peaceful Sunday morning. Earlier in the week, I had visited Bihać, a Muslim enclave which was also under constant shell-fire from the Serbs. Not many outsiders had managed to get into

Bihać at that stage, but I was able to spend a day with the small UN Military Observer team based there, commanded by a charming Irish colonel. He told me that he had had a meeting with the Serbian general attacking the enclave a few days before, during which the general had mentioned almost casually that his aim was to drive out the Muslims and replace them with Serbs. When the colonel asked him how many Muslims he thought that might be, he shrugged and said, 'About three hundred thousand.' Over one year later the Muslims were still hanging on but had started fighting among themselves, borrowing weapons from the Serbs, because the various factions could not agree on future policy. This is just another example of how confusing the situation can be. Because the press could not get into Bihać, the plight of its people had not been reported in the same way as in Sarajevo at that time. It was an extraordinary feeling to be making these sorties into places where full-scale battles were under way, and then to return to Zagreb where life went on as normal.

When we finally arrived at the distribution point, which was a warehouse, there was no one there. After we had waited around like sitting targets for what seemed like ages, someone eventually turned up to open the doors. I was amazed to find that they were actually angry with us for arriving early. I could not believe it. These UN soldiers from Canada had risked their lives to get supplies to the people and they were being harangued for being early. When the doors of the warehouse were finally opened we saw that it was stacked with food which was obviously not being distributed to the local citizens. By now I was becoming very angry, as were the Canadian soldiers, but the warehouse people were settling down to drink coffee, smoke cigarettes and apparently stage a 'go slow'. It was a tremendous eye-opener to me. Perhaps it was typical of what happens in some countries receiving aid, but as we drove back through the shell-fire I could not help wondering if the good people who had gathered together the food and sent it off had any idea how ungraciously it would be received at the other end.

To begin with I was stunned to hear how the people grumbled about the supplies, complaining that some packaged foods were out of date or asking why better things could not have been sent. Later, when I was on the receiving end of these sorts of gifts, I began to understand why these civilized European people felt insulted to be sent old and sometimes dirty things which had been thrown out by families in other countries, and to appreciate better how it felt to be constantly reliant on other people's generosity and to have to receive their cast-offs with endless gratitude.

'Mark?' I could tell from Marina's voice that there was something wrong the moment I lifted the phone.

'Hi, how are you? Are you back in Zagreb?'

'Yes, but I have to go into hospital.'

'What do you mean?'

'I have to go in for some tests. I think it is very serious.' She sounded frightened and worried. 'Could you come round to see me? I am with my aunt.'

This was the first I had heard of her being ill. John MacKinlay had remarked to me about some red marks which she had on her face, but I had dismissed them as being a bit of sunburn. I went straight round to the flat and found her in a bad state. Her skin looked much more flushed and I could tell from the way she moved that she had a lot of aches and pains in her muscles.

'In the past,' she eventually explained when we were sitting down calmly, 'I have been ill. It is my cancer. I have spent time in hospital before.'

'You never told me.'

She shrugged. 'It is very boring to talk about illness, and I hoped that it had gone away. But it has come back again and they want to do tests.'

I am not a medical man and I did not understand most of the things she told me. Only later was the disease Lupus mentioned, but the term meant nothing to me. I was dazed and hardly able to hear what Marina was saying. Amidst all the horror and destruction I had witnessed in Croatia and Bosnia, she had been like a ray of hope and strength. She had seemed so young and capable and strong in her white coat, able to calm other people and to help them overcome their injuries and illnesses. It seemed inconceivable that she might be dying and in need of help herself. Despite everything that had happened to her she still managed to be fresh and beautiful and optimistic, to continue caring for others when she had seen so much that should have made her despair of human nature. How could this wonderful young woman be dying of a disease when she had survived so many physical dangers and suffered so much hardship? I simply could not take it in.

'When do you have to go in?' I asked.

'Tomorrow.'

'I will come and see you in the evening.' All the strong feelings which I had been struggling to hold in check now flooded out. I had to do everything I could for her, I simply could not bear the thought of her suffering any more.

And so, every evening, after I finished work, I went into the hospital to visit her. The weather had become unbearably hot and oppressive, the sun beating down remorselessly on the flat roof above the top-floor room which she shared with one other patient. We used to go out and sit in the corridor with the windows open to try to get a little movement and coolness into the air. Whenever I arrived there would always be friends or relatives crowded round her, none of whom could speak any English. I would be left sitting on my own while they all chattered on, occasionally flashing back a smile and nod of recognition if anyone spoke to me. Mostly they ignored me, or watched me out of the corners of their eyes with puzzlement. No doubt they were highly intrigued to know who this old Englishman was who waited so patiently for them to leave.

I knew by now that I was very attracted to Marina but had

no way of knowing how she might feel about me or whether she even wanted me there at all. I regretted terribly not being able to speak Croatian, feeling a complete outsider, and I have continued to regret it. It is a very hard language to learn and I am not a natural linguist, even though I have managed to master Nepali over the years. All the time that I was in Croatia I was with people who were keen to improve their English, and Marina seemed reluctant to teach me new words in Croatian, preferring to act as my interpreter all the time. Perhaps she liked the feeling of having me need her. Life was certainly much easier when she was around in those early months. The language barrier was often an enormous disadvantage to me when I was trying to communicate with the locals and I should have done more about it.

Marina made no effort to involve me in conversation with the others round the bed or to do any translating, preferring to deal with them first so that they would go and leave us in peace to talk in English. Sometimes it would take up to two hours before we would be alone and able to chat, and sometimes I would sit there almost all night, just holding her hand and waiting for her to fall asleep. I used to look forward to the moment of parting because then I would have an excuse to kiss her goodbye on the cheek. It was while I was saying goodbye to her one night that I first told her I loved her. She made no comment.

'They have done many more tests,' Marina said one evening as we both sat in chairs either side of the windows with the net curtains billowing in the welcome breeze. 'I think I am not going to be here much longer.' I saw that tears were beginning to well in her eyes and she was having trouble controlling her voice. I did not interrupt her and slowly she told me about her life. All the while she smoked endless cigarettes. I have never liked smoking, but it did not bother me now.

'Before I came to Lipik I was married,' Marina said, and I was shocked to feel an unfamiliar pang of jealousy somewhere deep inside me. 'He was a Serb, a doctor, a very suitable husband – before the war.' She gave a wry smile. 'Something happened when I was pregnant that gave me a great shock and I went into a coma. Ivan, my son, died just a few weeks after he was born.' She stopped talking and seemed to be gulping for air. 'It happened three years ago and this is the first time I have talked about him.' She paused again to compose herself. 'That is why the children in the home are important to me. I look at them and I imagine that that is what Ivan would have looked like by now, or how he would have looked in a few years' time. They have lost their parents and I have lost my child. We all needed each other. I love them, you see.'

She fell silent and I did not speak. She gazed out of the window and clung on to my hand, digging her nails in absent-mindedly, the tears now rolling down her cheeks.

'So I divorced my husband.' She suddenly spoke vehemently. 'I am a Catholic and I am supposed to feel guilty and ashamed about this, but as he was a Serb we were not married in a church. I don't feel guilty and ashamed because it was not my fault.

'In the war I saw so many children die, and such horrible deaths. But I still can't forget my own child. If I am going to die . . .'

'I'm sure you're not,' I blurted, and she put up her hand to silence me.

'If I am,' she continued calmly, 'I just want to do one more thing with my life.'

'What is that?'

'I want to find somebody to rebuild the children's home. I want to see the children come back to Lipik.'

We sat in silence for a while. I was confused by the emotions I was feeling. It seemed such a desperate plight and I could hardly bear the thought of her dying so unhappily. I was not experienced in handling such emotionally charged situations and I had no idea what to say. I tried clumsily to comfort her and then finally tore myself away and returned to Pleso Camp. The next night I came back again and we talked for another couple of hours. She had had the preliminary results, but they did not seem to have caused anyone to change their mind about her situation. Two nights after she told me her story I had made up my mind. As I left I made her a promise: 'I will rebuild the children's home for you.'

7

Home by Christmas

Marina had described to me how beautiful Lipik was in the winter, with the snow falling through the trees in the park, capping the little evergreen hedges and the Fontana. It was still only August, and in the overpowering heat of the hospital room we dreamed of how we would rebuild the children's home and see it together in the snow before I had to return to England. I was not due to go home until the end of December and in my mind that seemed like an age away. I wanted to give Marina a goal to help her through the coming months, something to live for, anything to help her out of her depression. She had had three terrible years with the loss of Ivan, the divorce, her illness, the war and the destruction of her town. I wanted to make it all up to her and this was all I could think of.

The following weekend Paddy Ashdown, the leader of the Liberal Democrats Party in England, came out on a fact-finding mission and I agreed to show him round. Part of my job seemed to be to act as a tour guide to anyone who passed through, but I was very happy to escort him as he used to be in the Royal Marines and would, I felt, be an interesting and interested visitor.

I was right. He particularly wanted to see refugee camps, and we drove to Slavonski Brod, which was constantly being attacked by Serb aircraft, although there were no airstrikes while we were there, and then on to a camp near Osijek. The camp was full mainly of women and children who had fled from Bosnia. They were crammed into small huts and tents and most of them were sitting inside to protect themselves from the burning sun, on makeshift beds. They were surrounded by the few possessions they had been able to bring with them when they were forced to flee their homes, away from the terror of Serbian atrocities. Many had not heard from their husbands, fathers, brothers and sons for several months and did not know what had happened to them. Paddy asked them if they would like to be evacuated to another country where they might be able to live in more comfort. All those we spoke to wanted to stay where they were, as close to their homes and menfolk as possible. They feared that if they went further away they would never see either again. It was a very humbling experience to sit among these proud people who had suffered and lost so much. On two occasions Paddy and I were moved quite literally to tears and had to beat a hasty retreat outside, blowing our noses on large handkerchiefs.

We stopped at a place called Đakovo on the way back to visit the cathedral where the nuns make their own wine and slivovic. Paddy and I spent a pleasant hour with the Mother Superior, sampling the wares. It was a particularly hot day and on the way back we stopped at Lipik for a cold drink.

I took Paddy to Jura's café in the centre of town. Jura was one of the strongest characters in the area. He was one of the thirty-five men who had defended the town against the Serbs and had lived to tell the tale. As soon as the Croats retook the town and he was able to get back, he re-opened his café, which became the main meeting place for the men of the town. It had an outside terrace with tables and chairs, where the locals who had returned to their devastated homes sat day in, day out, drinking, smoking, talking and roasting the occasional pig.

Paddy and I sat in the sunshine, chasing down the nuns' brews with some cold drinks, and I told him the story of the town and how it had been defended and recaptured and how the destruction which he could see all around him had happened. He could see the results in every direction. There was not a single house in sight which had not been wrecked. In the main street stood some handsome old mansions which must have been there for at least a hundred years. They had managed to withstand the coming of Communism, but the civil war had done for them. A few of the windows had been boarded up here and there, showing that people were returning and living where they could amongst the ruins, but the fabric of the buildings was hopelessly damaged, and the overgrown gardens threatened to smother what was left.

'What are you going to do after you leave here?' Paddy asked eventually.

'I don't know.' It was a question which I had been pushing to the back of my mind, distracting myself with adventures in Sarajevo. I certainly didn't feel ready to make any decision now.

'Well, if there is ever anything I can do, just let me know. I would be delighted to try to help you.'

'Thank you.' I was genuinely grateful for the offer. I had a feeling that I would need all the help I could get if I was going to keep my promise to Marina. I was still unsure how we were going to start on the project, so I decided not to mention it until I had a clear plan of action and knew exactly what I needed. I had enjoyed Paddy Ashdown's visit. We had hit it off immediately: he was somebody I had no trouble in understanding and relating to. That evening I dashed back to see Marina, excitedly telling her that I had been out to Lipik again and passing on the greetings of Jura and the other men at the café.

As soon as Paddy left, the Chief of the General Staff (CGS), General Sir Peter Inge, arrived with a large party of 'hangers-on' for a hectic visit. He was interested in the prospect of deploying a force into Bosnia and he wanted to meet all the top people. I took him on the same visit to Sector North as I had made with the Commander-in-Chief a few weeks earlier. We stopped at the same sad, deserted village for a picnic lunch, but this time the food was a lot better! Afterwards we strolled around and the Military Assistant (MA) took some photographs of the destroyed church. Seemingly from nowhere there appeared a very sullen, unsmiling and irate Serbian soldier who demanded that he be given the film from the camera. The Serbs were extremely sensitive about anyone taking photographs of the destruction they had caused. The CGS also became very irate, and I watched, amused, from the sidelines as the two of them argued. The Serbs clearly had no respect for British generals and the film was reluctantly taken out of the camera and handed over.

With an unwise display of anger the CGS told us all to get into the vehicles and we left in an undignified huff. About five miles down the road we were stopped by a Serbian roadblock and it was obvious that our friend had radioed through and told them to stop and delay us. They then proceeded to check all our papers slowly and were delighted when they found that one of our party, a brigadier, had only a photostat copy of his photo on his UN identity card, which, they said, made it invalid. We were helpless as we sat in our cars with our temperatures rising. Eventually, presumably when they considered that they had caused us enough inconvenience, they let us go. The Serbs had won another small but irritating victory over the UN. Secretly I was pleased that the CGS had been subjected to this humiliating treatment so that he could better understand our problems when dealing with the Serbs.

We organized his evening with us so that he could meet all the British troops in Pleso Camp: first drinks with the men in their club, then more drinks with the warrant officers and sergeants in their mess, followed by an excellent candlelit dinner on the basketball court outside the officers' sleeping accommodation – we had no mess. I drove back to the Intercontinental Hotel in Zagreb with him at about midnight and arranged to pick him up at six in the morning to fly to Sarajevo. I then went back to Pleso and rejoined the party, which was now more relaxed and in full swing.

I was shaken awake by my driver at 5.45 and it was at least a fifteen-minute drive to the hotel! We went through every red light in Zagreb and arrived, trying to look relaxed, as the general came through the front door at exactly six o'clock. Had I been one minute later my army career would undoubtedly have ended much sooner than it did.

As the early morning mist lifted, we took off for Sarajevo. The general stood behind the pilot throughout the journey. As we turned west from the coast to begin our run in, we all put on our flak jackets as normal, in case any Serbs in the surrounding hills decided to take a pot shot at the plane. Then we swooped down on the runway, nose down, for a perfect landing. The RAF crews were universally acknowledged to be the best.

We were briefed on arrival by the Senior Military Observer in Sarajevo, a New Zealand lieutenant-colonel, who everyone agreed was completely 'shot away'. He had been in Sarajevo for several months and was very lucky to have survived as he travelled anywhere he wanted, talking to both sides. On one of my visits to the city I went with him to meet the Serbian general in the hills above the city who was responsible for the siege. It was a weird feeling to be with the besieged and desperate people one minute and with the perpetrator of the suffering ten minutes later. The colonel only had a few weeks to go before returning home and he was becoming fatalistic that he would not see the end of his term. I am happy to say that he did survive physically but it was clear to us all that he should have been withdrawn much earlier for his own sake.

He gave us the most extraordinary military briefing I have ever been to, every sentence punctuated by long pauses and heavy puffs on endless cigarettes. He had us all, the general especially, spellbound with his inside stories.

We flew into Sarajevo early the next morning for briefings, before climbing into a French armoured personnel carrier (APC) for a sight-seeing tour of the city. In the APC there was one window for the driver and a hatch in the roof for the general to put his head out while his MA and I sat in the back, unable to see anything. We had no idea what was happening when, after some time, the vehicle suddenly jerked to a halt and roared backwards, throwing us forward in our seats, screamed to a halt again and shot forward, this time cracking our heads against the back. The MA pulled the general down by his belt and asked what was going on. He informed us that we were being mortared: one bomb had landed on the road in front and another behind. The MA reminded the general that it was his duty, as the commander of the vehicle, to keep everyone else inside informed as to what was going on. It is unusual for the CGS to come under mortar-fire on the front line – his job usually means sitting in a nice safe office in Whitehall – but Sir Peter took it all very much in his stride.

Having been out in Croatia for a month, I decided to ring Mladen Grbin in Glasgow to let him know how I was getting on, as I had promised I would. After chatting for a while about the state of the country generally, I said, 'By the way, you might be interested to know that I have undertaken to rebuild an orphanage in a place called Lipik,' and I told him the story of how it had been destroyed and the children evacuated.

'This is the most remarkable coincidence,' he said. 'I am in the process of setting up a new charity. We have just achieved charitable status and we are launching it tomorrow. It is called SOS for Children, the Croatian and Bosnian Child War Victim Trust Fund. What you are doing is exactly the sort of project I want to get going in the area.'

'So could we work together on this?' I asked.

'I don't see why not.'

'Well, as you have already gone through all the legal processes of setting up a charity, why don't I work under the flag of SOS for Children? Then all the money we raise can go through the Trust and donors can get tax back and all that sort of thing. I don't like or understand money, and I certainly don't want to be accountable for large amounts of it. Would you handle all that for me?' I didn't really know what I was talking about, and had no idea where to start.

'Certainly. I think that will work very well.' This was to be one of many happy coincidences and lucky breaks which kept me going at the beginning, when the task seemed most daunting. Mladen frequently deflated my enthusiastic, amateurish optimism with doses of harsh reality. He was well aware of just how big the task that I was blithely and over-confidently entering into was, and often had cause to remind me of this.

'What is your next step going to be?' he asked.

'The first thing I need to know is whether it is going to be physically possible to rebuild the existing buildings, or whether we will have to pull them down and start again. I am very much afraid that they will tell me they are too badly damaged to be saved. I'm aware that starting from scratch might be the cheaper option in the long run, but they are such beautiful buildings, or at least they were, with so much sentimental and symbolic value to the area, that I am desperately keen to save them. I really need an expert to tell me what is possible.'

'I think I might be able to help you there,' Mladen said, and gave me the name of a civil engineer in Zagreb, whom I contacted immediately. He agreed to come out with me and look at the ruins with a colleague.

When we arrived at the site we were met by Goran Nikles, the Acting Director of the orphanage and the man who had looked after the children so bravely all through the war. This was the first time I had met him. His English was not too good at that stage, but I was impressed by his sincerity and kindness. He was a very gentle man who really seemed to want to see the children back where they belonged. While they were being looked after in Selce his job had been to stay in Lipik and try to clean things up in the ruins, a hopeless task for one man. He had been wandering round, stacking a few tiles here and a few bricks there, making no impression at all on the chaos. He seemed very relieved to find someone else to work alongside and share the burden with. We immediately struck up a good rapport, despite the language barrier.

We walked round with the civil engineers, who told us that it would be possible to build on the existing walls, which had remained firm despite the bombs. So at least we knew that the task was going to be physically possible, and we could see more clearly what we were aiming for.

The doctors had worked out a balanced programme of treatment for Marina. She was now classified as chronically ill and would have to continue taking drugs for the rest of her life, however long that might be. But now that they had found the right drugs for her she was able to come out of hospital and resume her normal life while she waited for the detailed results of her tests. She could not go into the sun, having to protect her skin all the time, and she could not drink alcohol with the drugs, but otherwise she could continue as normal, provided she took things carefully.

Her parents, whom I had met briefly, now asked if they could meet me at her aunt's flat, where they were all staying. I went along one evening in some trepidation. Neither of them spoke English, so Marina was doing the translating as usual. Her mother was obviously very concerned about my motives for making such an unusual promise. She asked me why I wanted to do this.

Marina translated her question and warned me, 'Be very carefully how you answer this,' a grammatical mistake she always made in English but which was so appealing that I never wanted to correct her.

With my palms sweating like some adolescent boy's, I chose my words very slowly. 'I have been deeply shocked by what I have seen out here and by the story of the children and their home. I have recently been thinking that I would like to do something to help other people. Before I came out to Croatia I was already trying to get into a charitable organization where I could work with children. So this is what I want to do for myself. I hope also that in doing this I will help

Marina to recover from her illness. I think she needs something to fight for and an interest in life.'

Her mother looked at me for a few moments and then nodded. 'Okay,' she said.

Marina also nodded as she lit another cigarette. 'Good answer,' she said, and the tense atmosphere immediately relaxed. Her father, a wise and experienced businessman, was also concerned about whether I knew what I was taking on.

'I don't think you know quite what you are getting yourself into,' he warned me through Marina. 'You are being very naive in your approach. There are many sharks out there waiting to take your money. You don't speak the language or understand Croatians and all our systems and bureaucracy. You could find yourself in a lot of trouble.' I had imagined there were going to be a lot of hurdles, but the fact that someone might cheat me of the money had not occurred to me. However, it was too late to go back on my word now.

Now that I had made my promise to Marina to rebuild the home, I realized that I actually had no idea how to make a start. All I had was a pile of rubble in the middle of a destroyed town and no experience in either the building trade or the business of raising money. What I did have, however, were contacts in the media. At that time all the reporters and journalists wanted to get into Sarajevo since that was where all the action was, and the only way to get there was by plane. Because I was Commander of the British Contingent they had to get permission from me before they could fly in on an RAF plane. I realized that this gave me quite a powerful lever for gaining publicity. A few days later, Tony Gallagher of the *Daily Mail* made a request for permission to go in and I asked if he would do something for me in return. I told him the story of the orphans. I did the same with the *Daily Telegraph* when they asked. Both of them thought it sounded like a really interesting story and suggested we meet in the Esplanade Hotel, which is one of the grandest hotels in

Zagreb, to discuss it. Marina and I went along one evening to meet them and told our story again.

'Why don't you hold a press conference?' one of them suggested.

'Brilliant idea,' another chimed in, 'and you could get some of the children up and we could get pictures of them bouncing on your knees. We'll organize the whole thing and get all the international press and television people there. They're all hanging around looking for things to write about anyway.'

At this point I could see Marina beginning to bristle. 'No,' she said firmly, 'the children are not monkeys in the zoo, to be dragged across the country and paraded out for the cameras.'

'Okay.' The reporters were obviously surprised by her reaction but quickly regrouped themselves. 'How about if we all went down to where the children are now and met them and took some pictures of them there, in their own environment?'

Marina weighed this up for a few moments and then nodded. 'Yes, that would be all right, just taking pictures of them in the place where they are. Yes.'

We all heaved a sigh of relief, except that at the back of my mind I knew that Selce, which was where the children were staying, was a hot, four-hour drive away, and Marina had only just come out of hospital.

'We'll have to go down very early in the morning,' I said, 'before it gets too hot. We could be there by ten if we left around six.'

They agreed, and a few days later I drove round to Marina's aunt's flat at six in the morning and rang the bell. There was no reply. I knocked loudly but still got no response. I was beginning to panic. Had something happened in the night? Had Marina been rushed back to hospital? What could I do about all the reporters, photographers and television camera crews who were waiting for us in the Esplanade Hotel?

Eventually the door opened and a dishevelled Marina peered sleepily out at me. 'Are you all right?' I asked.

'Yes, I was asleep. What time is it?'

'Okay.' I tried to keep calm. 'You get dressed and I'll go and round up everyone else and come back for you.' Now that I knew she was all right I was feeling rather annoyed. She was always a stickler for punctuality, upbraiding me if I was even five minutes late for a meeting. But I didn't want to cause any ill-feeling at the start of a day which was likely to be long and arduous for all of us, particularly her. Her parents were staying at the flat as well and they were very averse to the idea of her going out in the heat.

'Don't worry.' She gestured for me to go as they shouted at her from inside the hallway. 'I will be ready when you return.'

When I got back I forgave her immediately. She looked wonderful in a wide-brimmed straw hat and light, flowing clothes, like a figure from an Edwardian garden tea party. We drove in the *Daily Mail* car with Tony Gallagher and the photographer, Steve Back. The others had their own cars. The heat was building up by the time we got to Selce, and there were a lot of children around because school was out for the summer holidays. We were greeted by a sea of tanned, smiling, curious faces. They all seemed to want to talk at once and shake hands. Marina was overwhelmed by a mob of them clamouring to take turns to hug her and to tell her everything that had happened to them since they last saw her. Their affection for her was obvious. They knew that she had suffered just as they had, and I felt something of an outsider as I watched them all together, bonded by their terrible shared experiences and enjoying one another's company. I desperately wanted to make everything right for them all, to protect them from whatever might come.

It had been a year now since the orphanage had been attacked and I think that some of the children had come to fear that they had been forgotten now that they were so far from Lipik, crammed into a home that was not theirs. They were excited at receiving visitors who had remembered them and taken the trouble to travel to see them.

Tony and Steve were keen to get the children together quickly so that they could get their story and pictures and head back to Zagreb to file them for the next day's edition. Steve immediately showed his professional skill by picking out Vladek, a Croatian boy, and Valentina, a Muslim girl, from amongst the crowd and asking them to pose together, getting a shot that would symbolize the whole project over the coming months and be republished over and over again. It was a glorious picture.

The rest of the morning was chaos, with lots of photographs, filming and interviews. Then the media departed in a flurry of slamming doors, revving engines and shouted farewells to the waving children. The *Daily Mail* men had left us their car, so that we could come back later when the sun had gone down and the air had cooled. A relative calm settled over the children after that and I was able to get to know them a little. I played football with some of the boys, while Marina sat serenely under the trees in her hat, with groups of children coming to her, some with news, some with questions about Lipik, and some with problems which they wanted to share with her. All the time I was playing I watched her out of the corner of my eye, her face animated in conversation with them, one minute earnest, then scolding, then teasing and laughing.

Late in the afternoon I was sitting with Stanko, who at five was the youngest of the children, on my lap. He had a perpetual grin on his face, displaying his missing teeth and gums. He began to stroke the stubble which had grown on my face since our early start that morning. He looked startled and stroked me again and then again. Then he ran off and fetched his two brothers and brought them over, making them stroke my face as he had. They all dissolved into giggles and it occurred to me that they had probably never felt a man's stubbly chin since they had no father. There was only one male teacher in the school, a rather forbidding, stern, elderly man who would not have encouraged such intimacy from the children. It felt good to be able to give them something they had not had before.

At the end of the day we called all the children together so that I could talk to them through Marina. 'It has been lovely to meet you all today,' I said, waiting for her to translate, watching their faces as they stared up at me, one or two of the little ones already distracting each other. 'We have come down here because I want to bring you news about Lipik. I want to make a promise to you that I will rebuild your home so that it is even better than it was before it was destroyed.'

Some of the children jabbered at Marina after she had translated, and she turned to me. 'They want to know when you will rebuild it by.'

'Tell them,' I said grandly, 'that they will be home by Christmas.'

'Which Christmas?'

'Er . . . this Christmas, of course.'

I felt elated as we got back into the car and headed home that evening. The children had been wonderful, so welcoming, so joyful and excited, not at all how I had always imagined orphans in war-torn countries to be. Marina was quiet, so I did not interrupt her thoughts. I imagined she might fall asleep quite soon.

'I don't think you can rebuild it by this Christmas,' she said eventually.

'Why not?'

'There is a lot to do. You have to raise the money, deal with the Government and all the other officials to get permissions. You have to get plans drawn up and then you have to actually build it. I don't think four months is quite enough.'

When she put it like that it did sound rather a tall order. Having been in the army all my life, I was used to being able to get things done very quickly because there were always hundreds, and sometimes thousands, of people ready and able to do whatever you told them. This was going to be very different. I was on my own. Yet I never had any doubt that, however long it took, we would eventually overcome all the problems.

8

On To the World News

Just before we went down to Selce to meet the children, I remembered that Martin Bell was still in Sarajevo. He was someone who I felt could do a lot to help our cause. If the orphanage project was mentioned on the BBC News it would immediately reach millions of people, including all the other media, who might then become interested in the story. It seemed like a contact well worth following up.

I was due to make a trip there anyway, so I sent a message to tell Martin I was flying to Sarajevo the next day and asking if I could see him while I was there. We had some Royal Engineers down there at the time. They were constructing observation posts for the UN observers who were in very exposed positions, often directly on the Serbian and Muslim gunlines surrounding the city, with no protection from incoming fire. It was a very dangerous job for the Engineers because they too were being shot at as they worked. Questions were being asked back in Britain as to whether our troops were being put in unnecessary danger, so I wanted to make sure that they were being given as much protection as was possible under the circumstances.

While I was talking to the Engineers, Martin Bell wandered in, looking highly conspicuous in his white suit. He invited me for a cup of tea in the basement garage of the Post Office which the UN had occupied as its headquarters and where all the television companies had crammed their equipment in to create makeshift studios. I have never seen so much expensive electronic gadgetry in such a small and inappropriate place. It was a lovely morning, so we sat outside in the sun on rickety old chairs while I told the story of the orphanage once again.

'Can you come to Lipik?' I asked eventually. 'Because if you could get out there and do a report on the town and tell the story of the orphanage I'm sure the money would start to come in.'

'I really don't think that I dare leave Sarajevo just now,' he said. 'If I was up in Lipik at the moment when something happened down here my bosses would be jumping up and down, demanding to know what I was playing at. I will tell you what I'll do, I'll give you the names of one or two people who could help you, other reporters and stringers who I know are in Zagreb at the moment. It's a great story, I'm sure you'll be able to get coverage.'

He found a piece of paper and started to write down names for me. At that moment somebody came rushing up shouting, 'There's a hell of a fight going on downtown.'

Martin immediately forgot about making my list. 'Right,' he said, 'come on, let's go and see what's going on.'

I followed him out and we climbed into his armour-plated BBC Land-Rover. Martin drove, with his cameraman and soundman in the back. We tried to locate the trouble by the columns of smoke going up into the air. Following the grey plumes down the back-streets, we eventually found the scene of the action in a street where some shells had landed. There were cars burning and wounded people lying on the pavements being tended by friends and relatives. We got out and Martin looked around.

'I think the real action is a bit further over there,' he decided, so we climbed back into the Land-Rover and headed on until he found an area where the fighting was still under way, with bullets and shells flying in all directions. We stopped in a deserted car park and got out again. The cameraman started whirring away and the soundman pointed his microphone, which looked like a strange sort of furry ferret on a pole, up towards the passing bullets to try to catch the effect of the noise all around us. Martin was wandering about, trying to see what was happening, and I found myself mindlessly following him. The thought occurred to me that I was not actually behaving much like a professional soldier. We are trained to take cover when there is live ammunition hurtling around and if it is effective – in other words, if there is a good chance of being hit. The last thing I would do in such a situation is stroll around in a white suit in full view of the enemy. This incoming fire seemed reasonably effective to me, but I didn't feel that I could start hiding behind things if Martin and his colleagues were not. I looked around and saw that we were the only people still out in the open. An old woman was cowering in a doorway a few yards away. She looked so terrified that I was tempted to take off my flak jacket and give it to her.

An experienced reporter like Martin has seen many more wars than most professional soldiers, but he had confided to me at our last meeting in Sarajevo that he considered this the most dangerous war for the media that he had ever covered. So much random fire from artillery, mortars, machine-guns and snipers was going on all the time. There was never any way of knowing where the fire would come from next, so it was almost impossible to take effective precautions. 'You know,' the cameraman said casually as we stood in the middle of the car park, 'I think it's possible that we have become the targets. I think they are actually aiming at us now.'

'Hmm,' Martin mused thoughtfully. 'I think I might go and put my flak jacket on.'

'Now I know it's serious,' I half-joked, knowing that he didn't normally bother with such things, even though I had had mine on, and my helmet, since arriving in Sarajevo.

He strolled back to the Land-Rover to put on the flak jacket under his jacket, and I accompanied him nervously. He then wandered off again and I thought I might stand with my back to the Land-Rover, so that at least I would be covered from one side, when a series of mighty explosions went off right beside us as a line of mortar bombs crashed across the car park past the Land-Rover. Martin was thrown to the ground. The cameraman continued filming the whole time as the soundman and I ran over to help him.

'I'm hit,' Martin said matter-of-factly, as if for the camera's benefit. 'I'm alive. I'll survive.'

'Get him to the Land-Rover,' I shouted, and we began to drag and lift him over. 'Who's got the keys?'

'I have,' Martin muttered, putting his hand into his pocket. 'Can't find them. They must have fallen out.' After what seemed like an age of hunting around we found them on the ground where they had fallen out of his pocket.

He had been hit below the level of his flak jacket and we were able to get a first field dressing on to his groin and lower abdomen. There was not too much blood, which seemed hopeful. It was the first time in my military career that I had ever had to put a first field dressing on while under fire. All those years I had been carrying them around, but we actually used a BBC one.

The soundman took the wheel of the Land-Rover, pressed his foot to the floor and pointed its nose towards the UN building on the other side of town. I thought there was a strong possibility we would all die in a crash long before we got there. When we arrived back an emergency team ran out with a stretcher to take Martin to the field hospital, and the rest of the media crowded round to try to find out what was going on.

Someone else from BBC News came up to me. 'Would you mind going on the One o'Clock News live, Colonel Cook,' he asked, 'to tell what happened to Martin?'

'Sure, why not?' It was a few moments before I realized just what was being handed to me on a plate. As all the other reporters and camera crews began to join the queue to record my story, I realized that I was actually going to be able to tell millions of people about the orphanage project directly, right in the middle of what would probably be the most watched and talked-about event of the day in Britain.

'May I just ring my wife?' I said. 'Because if she hears the news before she has heard from me it might be a bit worrying for her.'

'Of course, no problem.' A satellite telephone was produced and I was struck by how much better equipped than the army the media are. I was instantly through to Caroline at home. I explained that I was all right but would be on the News in half an hour. I asked her to tell headquarters at Wilton about it so that they were warned in advance.

'What were you doing in Sarajevo?' she asked, puzzled.

'I came down to see the Royal Engineers who are here, and to talk to Martin Bell. I'm trying to get his support for a project which I have taken on for rebuilding an orphanage in Croatia.' This was the first time I had mentioned the idea to her and she seemed to take it in her stride.

At that point I had to say goodbye because they wanted to clear the lines and get ready for the broadcast. They equipped me with an earpiece and I could hear the studio in London talking to me, telling me what was happening. 'We're now going over live to Colonel Cook,' I heard the newscaster's voice in my ear. 'Hallo, Colonel Cook. Can you tell us what happened?'

I proceeded to tell the story and answer a few follow-up questions. 'Actually,' I said, before I could be cut off by the newsreader in London, 'I came down here because Martin and I went to school together and I wanted to see him about a project which I've got for rebuilding an orphanage in a place called Lipik.'

The message got across live to millions. It seemed that, thanks to Martin taking a direct hit in the groin, we had had our second lucky break. We now had a charity set up and running and a huge publicity plug. It seemed to me that providence really must be on our side – if not on poor Martin's. It was yet another twist of fate; I had gone to Sarajevo to ask him if he would do a report for television on Lipik, and instead I had appeared on TV talking about him. A few days later the *Daily Mail* carried a wonderful article about the children, using Steve Back's picture of Vladek and Valentina, and a picture of Marina and me sitting among all the children at the orphanage, which reinforced the idea of the project in the public's consciousness.

The French medical team dealt with Martin in Sarajevo and then we took him back to Zagreb in a Hercules and held him in our first-aid unit until he could be flown back to Britain late that evening in a Medivac plane, sent out by the BBC and bristling with doctors, specialists, nurses and equipment.

As far as the media were concerned, I had now become the man who 'rescued injured BBC reporter Martin Bell from the fighting in Sarajevo'. The reach of the international media was brought home to me when I received two letters a few weeks later, one from Darjeeling and one from Katmandu, from clerks who had worked for me in the Gurkhas, both of whom had seen me on television the night before and wanted to know what I was up to.

Caroline had also been studying the story in the *Daily Mail*, and something about the picture of Marina and me with the children had rung a distant alarm bell.

'I saw the article in the *Mail*,' she told me on the telephone that evening.

'Oh, yes, isn't it wonderful publicity?'

There was a long pause at the other end of the line. 'And . . . ?' she said eventually.

I realized immediately what Caroline was getting at. 'And what?' I probably sounded flustered, although at that point I had not done anything to feel guilty about. However, after so long together Caroline seems virtually able to read my mind, as I can hers.

'And . . . ?'

'I don't know what you are talking about.'

'And what about Dr Topić?'

I knew that I had to play it down, and started explaining how she was the local doctor and how involved she was with

79

the children, but when I finally hung up I felt breathless and horribly guilty. I hadn't lied, but I hadn't been open and I hated that. Something told me that I was starting down a slippery slope and I had no idea how to arrest my descent.

So now we were ready to do some serious fund-raising. I had made some very rough calculations in my head and I thought that we would probably need about £250,000 to complete the project – perhaps £100,000 for each of the main buildings and £50,000 for the kitchen and dining room building. We would then fill it with second-hand furniture donated by kind sponsors ... I was still a complete innocent in the business, but I was soon to learn.

9

Deeds Not Words

Marina's parents had come up from Mostar to help her to repair her flat in Lipik so that she could move out of the hospital into a place of her own. Structurally the block of flats, which was one of a pair, was still all right. It must have been an ugly piece of architecture even when it was new, a typical 1960s high-rise concrete block, erected as swiftly and as cheaply as possible, overwhelmingly black and grey and depressing. Rats could be seen disappearing into holes in the wall on the dingy concrete staircase, and everyone could hear everything that went on on the floors above and below them. It had not, however, sustained a direct hit, and although it was the sort of eyesore that people would be petitioning the local government about in most countries, it was being patched up to provide the best housing in town. Goran's flat, by contrast, was part of an elegant old town house overlooking the railway line at the back of the town, but it still had no running water, whereas Marina's flat was due to have hot and cold water installed once the pipes had been relaid.

All the windows in the block had been blown out and all Marina's possessions had been looted. Her white doctor's coat had been pinned to the wall with threats smeared across it in human blood, but this damage was gradually being cleared up. Her parents were repairing the bullet-holes in the walls and window-frames, replastering and painting, replacing the locks on the door and the glass in the windows. She was being given new furniture by the Red Cross and had received other gifts like a cooker and a fridge from well-wishers.

The flat was basically one small room, with a kitchen big enough for a table and chairs, some floorspace for the occasional guest, and – that most precious of assets – a bathroom. There was still no water and no gas, but there was a bare electric lightbulb to see by – the first step on the road back to a civilized life.

While her parents were working in Lipik, Marina continued to stay with her aunt in Zagreb, and every evening I would go round to visit her. She was still waiting for the results of her tests and was very worried. Several times I sat up all night with her, holding her hand until she fell asleep, while her aunt slept in the room next door. When she finally drifted off in the early hours of the morning I would slip out and return to Pleso Camp.

For days on end I hardly slept myself and I was turning up for work like a zombie, drained both emotionally and physically. I realized that I was in danger of not doing my job well and decided I should take my Chief of Staff, Major Martin Drake, into my confidence, so that he could watch out to ensure that I didn't make any major mistakes. I told him about Marina and how she was passing through a very dark time in her life, and explained that I was trying to help her by making this commitment to rebuild the children's home.

'You should keep a record of everything that happens,' he suggested, 'so that you can write a book at the end of it.' I laughed at the suggestion and gave it no more thought.

When the results of Marina's tests did finally arrive they did not appear to change the doctors' minds about the gravity of her illness. Everything seemed to depend on how well the drugs continued to work.

When her parents had finished their work I moved Marina back to Lipik in a Land-Rover, with her clothes and medical books and the few other possessions she had been able to salvage from her previous homes. There was still no running water or gas in the block, and as she was not strong enough to fetch and carry buckets for herself, I made it my responsibility to ensure she always had enough water, driving up every other day, carrying buckets and jerry-cans from a standpipe at the hospital, and bringing drinking water up from Zagreb with me. I enjoyed looking after her and helping her to rebuild her life, although I realized that I was getting enmeshed and she was becoming reliant on me. I could not imagine how I would ever disentangle myself from her, so I put the matter to the back of my mind and continued to live from day to day.

I decided that if we were going to be asking people for money we needed some photographs of the orphanage in its ruined state, so I took Sergeant Tomlinson, a Royal Air Force photographer in my headquarters, up with me from Pleso and we went to meet Marina at the flat. Some children were playing with an old Russian 66-mm rocket launcher on the steps outside. The hallway inside was dark and threatening. Although her parents had finished doing all the repairs for her, the flat was still an empty shell with just a few hard chairs to sit on.

'You should meet the Mayor of Lipik,' Marina said to me as we sat drinking coffee, 'to tell him what you are doing. He lives just upstairs because his house was destroyed too. I will fetch him.'

A few minutes later she reappeared with Marino the Mayor, a burly young electrician. He had been one of the thirty-five defenders of Lipik and, like most of the survivors, had been badly wounded, spending weeks in hospital. He was now working hard to try to bring some life back to the place and organize the few people who had returned.

'This is Colonel Mark Cook,' Marina introduced us, 'and he has promised to rebuild the orphanage for us.'

We talked for a while about the project, and the more enthusiastic I became, the more bored Marino the Mayor seemed to be as he chain-smoked, nodding his head wisely but saying nothing, and frequently looking out of the window or down at the floor, where he was shuffling his feet. After a while we decided to go out and walk around the grounds so that the photographer could get his shots of the ruins in the late afternoon light. As we left the flats, the children with the rocket launcher came running over and Marino, their father, ruffled their hair and beamed proudly.

When it finally became too dark to take any more pictures, we wandered down to Jura's café and sat outside with some cold beers. My enthusiasm was beginning to wane in the face of Marino's weary, polite indifference. Eventually, when the beer had refreshed him, he leaned over to me, with Marina still translating. 'Colonel Cook,' he said, 'if you really mean what you say, please will you do something to show us? Because we have many people coming here, taking photographs and saying they are going to help us, and we never see them again. We are tired of empty promises. So please, if you mean it, do something to show your good faith. We need some deeds, not just more words.'

He was giving me a challenge and I liked that. I like someone to say 'Prove it' to me, so that I can really get going. I was confident that we would succeed in the end, but I had to find an effective way to get started. It was no good waiting for some miracle to happen as a result of the news broadcast and press coverage, I had to take a more immediate and practical step. All the way back to Pleso I kept turning the problem over in my mind. There were certainly quite a few people I could write to, like Peter Praxmarer and Paddy Ashdown, but that was all too vague and too far in the future. If I was to meet Marino the Mayor again in a few weeks and he asked me how I was getting on, I could hardly tell him that everything was going fine because 'I've written a lot of letters'. That would merely confirm all his worst fears.

As I lay in bed that night I had an idea – ask the Regimental Sergeant Major, of course. That is what you do when you have a problem in the army. RSMs are always the best at getting things sorted out.

As soon as I had the pictures from Sergeant Tomlinson I called the RSM in, showed them to him and told him the story. 'Do you think it would be possible to get some volunteers together,' I said, 'to go up to Lipik this weekend and start clearing the rubble? I think we need about twenty men.'

'Right, sir, leave it to me.'

A couple of hours later he was back. 'Got 'em, sir.'

'Are you sure they're all volunteers, RSM?' I asked suspiciously.

'Oh yes, sir, all very keen,' he assured me.

'All right, then. Tell them I'll meet them in front of the headquarters building at lunch-time on Saturday.' This week-end was going to be the first since Marina moved back into the flat full-time, and I was looking forward to seeing her and showing her that we were starting to carry out the promise.

On Saturday morning the post brought our first donation, a cheque for £500 from Martin Bell in gratitude for what I had done for him in Sarajevo. It was a wonderful start. The heat was tremendous that day and I thought I had better take up something for the men to drink, so I bought four crates of beer from the canteen. Then I noticed that they were loading crates of their own on to their four-tonner. When we arrived at Lipik, Goran had also laid on beer, so by the time we were ready to start work there was a beer mountain and I began to feel very doubtful about whether the men would be in any state to do anything.

We arrived soon after lunch. Many of the men had never been out of Pleso Camp since arriving and they were pretty shocked by what they saw all around them. I sat them down facing the ruin and briefed them on the story so far. 'I have made this promise to the children to rebuild their home for them,' I said, 'and the first step is to start clearing out the rubble so that building work can begin as soon as we have raised the money. This is work that has to be done manually because, as you can see, there is no room to get machines inside the old walls to do it. If we can do this ourselves it will save money and time. It will also signal our intentions to the local people. They are not too impressed with the UN or with the British at the moment. They think we talk a lot and don't do much, and to an embarrassingly large extent they are right.'

All the time I was talking I was aware of the beer mountain behind them, and I had this horrible vision that the moment I said, 'Right, let's go', they were going to head straight for the crates. I had not had much experience with British soldiers, having spent most of my service with Gurkhas. In my mind Gurkhas were the best soldiers in the world and I was wishing I had them with me now.

As I was coming to the end of my talk I could see that they were getting restless and shuffling around. 'So has anyone any questions?' I asked.

After a moment's silence Warrant Officer Watson bawled out, 'Right-ho, lads, let's go!' and they shot off to the main building with picks and shovels, straight past the beer mountain. As the sweat began to flow they started to drink gallons of water, and didn't even look at the beer. Goran could not believe his eyes and kept begging them to slow down and offering huge pots of viscous Croatian coffee, produced by a woman from the ruins of a neighbouring house and by Marina from the hospital kitchen. It was much stronger than anything most of the men had ever tasted before, with inches of brown mud in the bottom, which we were told were called *zots* in Croatian, and one or two of them nearly choked. Goran seemed frightened they were going to do themselves injuries in the heat, but as the afternoon wore on they worked faster and faster. It was the hardest possible physical labour. Obviously a lot of them had been bored back at camp and this challenge was exactly what they wanted. Marina spent the afternoon like Little Red Riding Hood with her basket, bringing coffee and cold drinks over in relays, joking with the men and urging them on to ever greater heights of activity.

Because the rooms were not that big we divided them up into groups of three or four and it was not long before the competitive urge took hold and they started racing each other, seeing who could clear their room first. Each room could take up to five or six hours of flat-out work to complete.

All through that first day we worked like mad. It was fun. As soon as dusk came we started to drink the beer. I had warned the men that as far as I knew there was no hot running water yet in Lipik and I had no idea where they would be sleeping. As a result they had all brought camp beds and sleeping bags with them so that they could camp down somewhere in the ruins of the hospital.

Marina told me she had made some arrangements, and as it was getting dark she offered to show the men where they were sleeping, leading them to a spiral fire-escape at the back of the hospital, past wrecked ambulances and old broken beds which had been scattered in all directions. At the top of the fire-escape she showed them into a room containing twenty hospital beds splendidly made up with big, crisp white sheets and pillows, and the men's eyes nearly popped out of their heads. She then showed them the hot showers, which were supplied with scalding spa water directly from the thermal springs under the building. They felt they were being well rewarded for their labours.

Once they had cleaned themselves up we all went down to Jura's café and sat under the trees drinking more beer and talking. At one stage I stood up to say a few words of gratitude, and I held up Martin Bell's cheque to show them that the project really was up and running. It was a tremendously generous donation for one man to make and it stoked up our mood of optimism – if things went on like this we would have all the money we needed within a month or two.

That night I stayed at Marina's flat and our relationship changed irrevocably. Both of us knew that it was a dangerous line to cross but we were unable to resist the temptation. Living in a place like Croatia, where there is so much death and suffering, makes one very fatalistic about life. We had no idea how things would turn out, so we just decided to let fate take its course. From then on I was starting to tell lies and cover up and nothing was ever going to be the same again.

I quite expected the men to spend the next morning in bed. I have to say that they did not get up at the crack of dawn, being in really comfortable beds for the first time in months, but they were back at work before many other forms of life had appeared on the streets. All through Sunday they worked at the same feverish pace, only stopping for lunch in the hospital before working on until it was dark again. I was concerned that they would get back to Pleso too late for supper but they were not worried, assuring me they would pick up some pizzas in Zagreb on the way back.

What they had achieved that weekend was a pin-prick in the chaos, but the results were satisfyingly clear to see. The task had been to dig the rubble out of the rooms, loading it into wheelbarrows, running them up ramps and shooting it out of the windows, which had no glass left in them, so that it could be cleared away by machine later. The debris included the roof and the second and third floors, complete with their smashed and burnt furnishings, twisted plumbing, shattered floors and ceilings, all of which had collapsed down on to the ground floor. It was a marathon task but all the volunteers wanted to come back the next weekend and bring their friends.

For Marina, Goran and me, those weekends early on in the project were the best time of the whole eighteen months that it went on for. One Saturday night Goran arranged for a pig to be cooked on a spit while we worked, for a barbecue feast in the evening. The atmosphere was tremendous and we all felt we were really doing something to help instead of just standing by and watching.

One weekend a reporter from a local paper came to see me. He was a dour, scowling chap with a heavy five o'clock shadow and dishevelled clothing. I took him round and showed him what we were doing and he dutifully took notes. At the end he looked at me hard.

'Colonel Cook,' he said, 'does it not strike you as strange that you and twenty British soldiers are giving up your weekends to do this hard work for Lipik, when at least twenty strong local men spend their weekends sitting round the corner in Jura's café, drinking coffee and smoking cigarettes?'

The contrast had not occurred to me before and I had to think before I answered. 'I imagine,' I said at last, 'that when you have lost absolutely everything, and you are not even sure that the whole thing won't happen again just when you have rebuilt your life, it must be very hard to find the motivation to do this sort of work. For us it is a challenge, but it is not our whole lives. I think that must be the difference.' I am not sure that I convinced him.

Marina suggested that we needed a brochure to send out to people and said that she had a friend in Zagreb who was into printing and design. This was an excellent idea as I was writing to many people and companies asking for money or help in kind. Mario Cvirn, her friend, came up to see us and we liked his suggestions very much. We eventually ordered 1,000 colour brochures. They cost £2,000, which we did not actually have at the time because we were waiting for promised donations to arrive, but I was determined to keep things moving. It was a simply designed, six-page brochure with one colour photograph on each page and very few words. It told the story quickly and clearly, which I thought important when trying to get money from busy people. It had the lovely photo of Vladek and Valentina on the front, with the toothless Stanko wearing my UN beret on the back, and the one word 'help' under the picture. It turned out to be a wonderful investment.

On 17 September, Marina's birthday, the *Sunday Telegraph* sent a photographer all the way over from Slavonski Brod, a town about fifty miles away which was constantly under fire, to take a picture of me in the ruins of the orphanage, so I drove up from Zagreb to meet him. My hands had been very battered about by concrete and rubble and one of my fingers had become alarmingly infected. When the photographer had left I went to show my finger to Marina, who was on duty at the hospital.

'I will have to lance it,' she said. 'It is very bad. I need to cut it.'

It was an agonizing few minutes for me and I could see that she did not enjoy doing it at all. When she finished she looked up at me.

'Now I know.'

'Know what?'

'Now I know how much I love you. Normally to do this to a patient would not worry me, but hurting you was the most difficult thing I have ever had to do.'

10

Governments and Other Heroes

During the week, when we were not working on the site, I was writing letters to anyone I could think of. One of the first was to Paddy Ashdown to remind him of his promise of assistance should I ever need it. I told him about my idea and asked for his help. He wrote back immediately with some suggestions and copied my letter to Baroness Chalker, who was Minister for Overseas Development. A few days later I received a call from the British Embassy in Zagreb.

'Baroness Chalker is coming out to Croatia next week,' I was told. 'She has expressed a wish to meet you. Would you be able to come to a dinner at the Esplanade Hotel so that you can be introduced to her?'

'Of course.' I was surprised and delighted – it seemed Paddy had come up trumps. 'Just tell me when.'

'We'll send over an official invitation.'

The invitation duly arrived and the guests all met for drinks before dinner at the elegant old hotel. Baroness Chalker was late because she had been travelling around the country all day. 'I've put you next to the minister at dinner,' the ambassador, Bryan Sparrow, told me, 'with Mr Whitlam, the head of the British Red Cross who has come out with her, on the other side of you. That gives you two people to nobble.'

I was immensely grateful for what was the first of many acts of great personal kindness that Bryan Sparrow and his wife showed me over the next eighteen months. I intended to make full use of the opportunity he was offering me. When we were finally seated in the grand dining room, beneath the chandeliers and paintings, Baroness Chalker turned to me. 'So, Colonel Cook, tell me about this project of yours.'

I told her the story. 'Would you like to see some photo-graphs some time?' I asked.

'Yes, I would be very interested.'

'Good.' I reached for the envelope of pictures which I had slipped under my seat as we came in and proceeded to lay them out in front of her among the sparkling wine glasses and cutlery.

She quickly recovered from her initial surprise and studied the photographs which Sergeant Tomlinson had taken. 'You know, it's not usual for the Government just to hand out money for *ad hoc* projects like this,' she said, and my heart sank, 'but I think this is an exceptional case and we should be able to help you. If you write to me formally with all the details I'll see what I can do.'

She then went on to talk to the ambassador on her other side and I turned my attention to the head of the British Red Cross. He was equally interested and thought that they might be able to help, although in fact the Red Cross were never actually able to do anything for us, having too many other pressing projects in the area. As soon as I got to the office in the morning I wrote the letter to Baroness Chalker and imagined what a great help it would be if we received a Government donation to get us going.

Meanwhile private donations had started to come in as a result of the publicity. At about the time Martin Bell's cheque arrived, other people were contacting Caroline back in Eng-land. She was asked to do an interview for a local Salisbury newspaper and at the same time she met a reporter from BBC Radio Wiltshire Sound and was interviewed by him. A lady called Marika Edge, whom we had not seen for twenty years, heard Caroline being announced while fiddling with the car radio as she waited for her child in a car park. When she got home she looked us up in the telephone directory and called. She checked that we were the same Cooks she had known in Hong Kong and then said she would like to help with the appeal. She was Dutch by origin and had a family trust called the Anton Jurgens Trust which allocated a certain amount of money every year to charities. She said she would like to suggest to the trustees that the orphanage receive some of the money this year: by happy chance, their annual meeting was to take place the following week. She asked Caroline to send her all the details and hinted that we might get three or four thousand pounds, which sounded fantastic. The following week she rang back with the news that the trustees had decided to allocate the whole amount to us. 'You'll be getting a cheque for £25,000,' she said, 'and we may be able to repeat the amount again next year if you need it.'

This stroke of luck alerted me to the fact that there are hundreds of these trust funds in existence. Later, back in England, I went to the local library to look them all up so that I could write to the ones which supported our sort of cause. Unfortunately, however, we were not able to repeat our success on that front.

A few weeks later I received a reply to my letter from Baroness Chalker saying that the Overseas Development Administration were going to send me £100,000. This was like an official stamp of approval, and it meant that other people started to take notice of us. With the British soldiers doing the work and the British Government making a donation, the Croatian Government could see that I was really serious and did intend to carry out my promise. They began to make noises about making donations themselves. Meanwhile, we continued to work at weekends on clearing the site.

Sitting in Jura's café one Saturday evening with the soldiers and the usual group of local men, I heard the name of Fitzroy Maclean mentioned. Marina was translating for me as usual.

'Have they heard of Fitzroy Maclean?' I asked, surprised.

'Of course.' They all laughed. 'Everyone has heard of him. He is a great man. He helped us win the war and he set up Tito. He played a big part in creating post-war Yugoslavia. Everybody knows about him.'

'Have you ever met him?' I asked. This really made them

laugh. I might as well have asked if they had ever met the Pope or Abraham Lincoln. 'Would you like to meet him?' I persevered.

'If you can arrange that,' they said, almost choking with merriment, 'you can arrange anything.'

I decided that I would accept the challenge. I believed that if I could get Fitzroy to visit them it would really demonstrate that we were taking the plight of Lipik seriously. I knew that the Macleans were due to come out to their holiday home on the island of Korčula, and that made me think that I stood a chance.

The following day I tracked Fitzroy down in Trieste, on his way south. He was staying in a hotel and talking at a conference. I told him the story and asked if he could spare a day to come to Lipik to boost the morale of the locals and the soldiers and to improve the credibility of the British.

'Yes, yes, we'll see what we can do,' he said. 'I'm going down to Korčula tomorrow. Perhaps we could come back a day early and spend some time with you on the way home. Ring us in Korčula next week, will you?'

I did as he suggested and he and Lady Maclean agreed to fly up to Zagreb. At the same time there was a British recce party at the camp trying to get into some of the more inaccessible areas of Bosnia. The British Government had finally decided that they should do more to help in the area. Winter was approaching now and the whole of Bosnia and surrounding areas were awash with refugees. Something had to be done about getting aid to them or they would starve and freeze to death in the coming months. This party, led by Brigadier Miles Frisby, had arrived a week before. I had briefed them and then we had all set off in half a dozen assorted vehicles, in a totally self-contained convoy, complete with food and medical supplies, into uncharted territories where the UN had not yet been. Our mission was to attempt to get into the besieged town of Tuzla from the east, and to try to set up lines of communication so that relief convoys could get into central Bosnia.

I was told that the plan was to set up a new British force in Bosnia with me in command, which was why I was needed in the recce party. I thought at the time that the chances of us getting into Tuzla from Serbia in the east were pretty slim because we had to cross several front lines to get there, first through land captured by Serbs, back into Muslim areas for a few miles and then past more Serbs, but we had to try. We spent three or four days trying to get there, but with the endless roadblocks and checkpoints every few miles, each local warlord exercising his power to hold us up for hours on end, it became obvious we were not going to make it and we aborted the mission after a few days. We arrived back at Pleso Camp on Friday evening feeling tired and demoralized, to find orders from the UK to fly down to Split by Hercules aircraft the next day with our vehicles and try to get to Tuzla from the south-west. It was a longer route but did not involve crossing Serbian front lines. As Sir Fitzroy and Lady Maclean were due in the following morning I was not able to travel with the party, but agreed to follow the next day, once the Macleans' visit was over.

I met the Macleans off their plane from Split the following morning and took them to the briefing room where final preparations were being made for us to try to get into what had formerly been central Yugoslavia. It was a poignant moment when this old wartime commander, who had parachuted into the area during the last war, met the expedition of British troops preparing to go in nearly half a century later and compared notes in the operations room.

I asked Sir Fitzroy if he would present the Royal Engineers with their UN medals on a parade at Pleso before we went on to Lipik. A number of the Engineers subsequently received awards for bravery for their work in Sarajevo which I had put them in for and which they fully deserved.

There was a lot of media interest in Sir Fitzroy's visit, and after the ceremonies in Pleso I took him and Lady Maclean to lunch at the Esplanade Hotel, where I introduced them to Jeremy Bowen from the BBC, whom I had accompanied on a visit to the main hospital in Sarajevo a few weeks earlier. After lunch I drove them up to Lipik to watch the British soldiers hard at work. I had arranged to be there at four o'clock and arrived dead on time. The media had also all arrived and were waiting around the site, but there was no sign of any soldiers. I was deeply embarrassed and could not think what might have happened. I began to make frantic calls while the Macleans and the media waited patiently. There had been a hold-up which had prevented the soldiers from leaving the camp. Fortunately they turned up half an hour later and immediately started work with their normal energetic enthusiasm, so the photo-opportunity was able to go ahead, with Sir Fitzroy pictured digging alongside them.

The Macleans had agreed to stay the night in the hospital, in a room near to the men. That evening we threw a huge party at Jura's café, with all the local dignitaries invited to meet the great man. This was the first time I met Gordana, Goran's lovely wife, who has such a gentle nature and was always so kind to me despite great difficulties. There was a pig turning on one spit and a sheep on another and plenty of other food and wine. It was a wonderful evening. Both the Macleans spoke Croatian and talked to virtually everyone. Marina worked tirelessly as my translator. One of my officers, Mike Charlesworth, played the guitar and sang. He was joined by a Croatian violinist and we all sang British and Croatian songs late into the night, lit and warmed by the embers of the barbecues in the heart of the blackened and silent town. It was late September and still just warm enough to sit outside all evening. We danced under the trees, which had been decorated for the occasion with coloured lights, and forgot for a few hours the desolation all around as it vanished into the darkness.

That night, after taking the Macleans back to their room in

the hospital well after midnight, I drove back to Zagreb so that I could fly down to Split for the Tuzla expedition first thing in the morning. One of my officers was going to drive the Macleans back the following day to catch their plane. Unfortunately everyone forgot to tell them that the clocks were going back by an hour, so the next morning they got up at the appointed time and thought they had been deserted, with no breakfast ready and no one to meet them.

I knew nothing of this as I flew down to Split, joined the recce party and headed into central Bosnia. We visited all the places which were then still considered inaccessible. On the first day we stopped at a Bosnian brigade headquarters for discussions when, during a lull in the conversation, the commander said that he had read that an officer from Britain was planning to rebuild the orphanage in Lipik in Croatia. When I told him that it was me he stood up, shook my hand and said thank you with dignified gratitude. I received similar quiet, sincere thanks many times in the following months.

We decided where we were going to deploy the British troops and drew up a plan. It was an exciting week with a lot of tension and many shooting incidents. We passed by a burning Muslim village where every house had been deliberately set on fire. The Croatian commanders we met said the burning had been caused by Serbian shells, but it looked more like systematic arson and ethnic cleansing on the ground. Shells are never that precise in their targeting, and do not cause widespread fires. Now I could imagine how it must have looked in Lipik a year before, when all the houses were burning in every street.

The recce party was divided into several small groups, one of which came under attack from aircraft while visiting a hospital and one of our soldiers managed to revive an old man who had a heart attack. All the parties had tales to tell when we met up in the evenings. On one road, which was known to be a particularly dangerous sniper's alley, we all took our flak jackets off and pressed them up against the sides of the vehicles on the side where the Serbs would be firing from, to give ourselves extra protection as the drivers revved up and roared across the open space at full speed. I imagined how the children must have felt when they were being evacuated from Lipik in the lorry, lying piled up behind the sandbags as the rockets streamed past them.

The possibility of commanding this proposed new force of up to 2,000 troops in Bosnia was presenting me with a dilemma. Militarily it was a very exciting prospect. It would be a tremendous challenge, putting a shot of adrenalin into my army career at a time when it was apparently winding down. I was puzzled, however, as to where my staff and headquarters were going to come from in a matter of a few weeks. I certainly did not have enough people with me at Pleso. Anyone I voiced this doubt to told me not to worry, it would all be sorted out. I simply did not want to leave Marina, and the other problem was that if I was sent down to Split I would be miles away from Lipik and the orphanage and would have far too much work on my plate to be able to give the amount of time needed to fulfil my promise. If I left them now I was very much afraid that the project would grind to a halt and Marino the Mayor's early cynicism would have proved well founded. I felt I was being pulled in several directions at once. I decided there was nothing I could do to influence events just then, so I would have to wait and let fate take its course: a course of action, or rather inaction, I was to follow on many subsequent occasions when I was confronted by difficult personal decisions.

Rebel with a Cause

Brigadier David Jenkins, the Director of Military Operations in Whitehall and an old friend from Staff College, flew out to meet me and then we went to see General Philippe Morillon, the flamboyant Frenchman who had just been selected to be Commander of the Bosnian operation and who was to become a great media favourite. David wanted to tell me what had been decided at the Ministry of Defence and to discuss everything that was going to happen in Bosnia.

I went to the meeting in a state of considerable confusion. Either way the decision would affect the next part of my life dramatically. 'I'm sorry, Mark,' he told me, 'but we have decided that we need a complete brigade headquarters to run the operation in Bosnia, one that is already up and running. We are going to bring one in from Germany. We would like you to stay on in Croatia for the moment as COMBRITCON.'

I had to admit that it was the sensible decision but part of me felt a wave of disappointment. All along I had wondered why they were going to start a new headquarters from scratch for me when there were several redundant ones in Germany already up and running and about to be axed in the cuts. I knew this had been my last chance to go any further in the army. From now on it was almost certain to be back to an office job in Britain, time-serving until I either resigned or was made redundant. It brought back all the feelings I had been experiencing in England before I left, about wanting to move on to something else.

At the same time I felt an enormous relief, because now I could concentrate on fulfilling my promise to Marina and the children. Now that the whole emphasis of the war was moving to Bosnia, my job in Croatia would be even less demanding than it had been before. I could devote all my energies to the orphanage while serving out my time at Pleso Camp. Fate had again taken a hand to show me how things were meant to be.

David and I talked with General Morillon while he ate his lunch in his office. We were worried at the time about command and control of the British forces in Bosnia. Our generals in England wanted to put a brigadier in command of this battalion, basing him in Croatia at Split, while General Morillon was based in Bosnia. We thought this decision might upset General Morillon and were not looking forward to telling him about it. When we broke the news he simply shrugged.

'That's okay,' he said, 'I don't mind. You can have the Queen in Split as far as I'm concerned, it is no problem. No problem.'

Both David and I heaved sighs of relief, congratulating ourselves on having negotiated our way rather skilfully round that diplomatic minefield. Later in the conversation the new brigadier was mentioned again.

'Of course, I will have nothing to do with this brigadier of yours,' General Morillon said. 'He will be in Croatia and all the Bosnian forces will be under my command. That is why I don't care who you put into Split.'

This is just one small example of the command and control problems which have riddled the whole UN operation in that part of the world. Nobody can agree who commands and controls anything.

For nearly three months, since arriving in Croatia, I had worked non-stop, rushing from my job at Pleso back and forth to Marina and Lipik. I was exhausted and needed a break. My younger son William was about to go off on a round-the-world fishing adventure in his gap year before going to university. He had been planning the trip for over a year. He is a mad-keen fly fisherman and wanted to fish in as many countries as possible around the globe, earning a living wherever he could along the way. He had worked to earn the money for his air fare and was now heading for Chile, New Zealand, Australia and South Africa, planning to spend a few months in each country. I was very keen to see him before he went. My commanders in the UK reluctantly agreed that I could go home for four days over a long weekend. For some unknown reason they seemed to think that I should not be away from Croatia for too long in case something blew up. I have no idea what they thought was going to happen, or why they thought it would matter that I was a two-hour flight away. I could probably have got back to Zagreb quicker from England than I could have done from some parts of Croatia.

I was met at Heathrow by Caroline and William and we went home for a quiet weekend. It was lovely to see them both but I found it very hard to be away from Marina, even for those few days. On the Sunday we decided to attend a service at the church next to our house. The villagers were all very surprised to see me when we slipped in two minutes before the service started. We had deliberately not told anyone I was coming home, wanting to spend all the time together as a family. The vicar came straight over and whispered in my ear, 'Would you like to give a talk about what you are doing in Croatia, and we could donate the collection to the orphanage?'

It was an offer I could not very well refuse, so halfway through the service I went up and spoke for a few minutes, explaining what had happened in Lipik. I likened it to how life would be in the village if the Welsh suddenly invaded, tried to move everyone out and killed all those who stayed, burning every house to the ground. They got the biggest collection the vicar – who is Welsh – could remember. One of the congregation contacted me afterwards and told me that he was a member of the Honourable Company of Cutlers. He said they would like to donate a set of cutlery to the orphanage, in exchange for which he asked for some of the old cutlery for their museum. So when I got back to Lipik I hunted through the rubble for an old knife, fork and spoon to send off in exchange for some very nice Sheffield-made cutlery. He also gave me a personal cheque for £500 in memory of his son, and other people in the village gave large amounts. One of them, Anne Dixon, a particularly kind friend, used to be a house mistress at Sherborne Girls' School and this led to an invitation to be their guest speaker the following term; so the network expanded and the money started to flow in.

The weekend was a terrible strain for both Caroline and me, although I think we managed to hide it from William. I was terribly tense and looked exhausted, thin and drawn, or so everyone kept telling me. I had been under so much physical and mental strain. I seemed to be spending my whole time driving from one place to another, and on top of all that there was the guilt. Caroline could sense that something was wrong. I was withdrawn and unaffectionate, not acting like my normal self. She spoke to several of our friends about it and they all told her not to worry, that I was probably just emotionally drained from being in a war zone. Both of us were determined that William would go away confident that all was well at home, and really enjoy his year of adventure, so we put a brave face on it.

'Is there anyone else in your life?' Caroline once asked me when we were alone and when the tension became too great to ignore.

'No, of course not.'

'What about the pretty young doctor in the pictures?'

'No, certainly not.' And that was the first of many lies to come.

Sitting in the congregation of our little village church I was struck afresh by the contrast between my life in England and in Croatia. One weekend, when Marina and I had gone down to Selce to visit the children, we went to church. Slipping in quietly, Marina went to confession and I edged into one of the pews with the children. Their faces lit up at the sight of us and they all started whispering greetings and waving. The weather was warm and they were all in T-shirts; few of them had seen a hairbrush that day. As I sat with a grubby-faced, toothless, five-year-old Stanko grinning on my lap, Vladek and Daniel holding my hands and gazing up at me every time I sang or said a prayer, I looked around the church and saw on the other side several very smart middle-class families. Their children were all neatly turned out for church, hair brushed and faces scrubbed, particularly one rather sweet little girl dressed all in glowing white. They were looking across at the scruffy orphans with expressions of disdain mixed with pity. I felt very protective towards the urchins around me, and moved by their open displays of affection for me. It occurred to me then that all my life I had been on that side of the church. As a child I had always been cleaned up and put into a jacket and tie for Sunday worship, shoes shining and trousers pressed to razor-sharp creases. As an adult I had continued to dress like that and to bring my sons up to do the same. I realized that if it had been me on the other side of that church I would probably have been looking across at this motley crew of children with feelings of pity and smugness, imagining that if only they could they would want to be like me and my smart, clean family. I felt embarrassed at this view of myself and strangely comfortable in my new role on the scruffy side of the church. I realized that for nearly fifty years I had been labouring under a great many illusions. It was a shock. I gave the wriggling Stanko an extra hug and winked at Zdravko, who was trying to catch my attention from the pew in front.

After I returned to Croatia Caroline wrote me a long letter, asking me once again what was wrong and whether I had someone else in my life. 'I must know,' she said, 'please tell me the truth.' Whenever I had been away in the past we had always written to one another a lot. This time, partly because it was so easy to use the phone, I had lost the habit. Caroline had said at the weekend that she thought it was important we did communicate in writing as well as over the telephone. I did not know how to respond to her direct questioning, so I ignored the letter until the next time we were talking on the phone.

'What about what I asked in the letter?' she persisted. 'You haven't answered my question.'

'I didn't answer because I thought it was such a silly question.' I tried to laugh her out of insisting on an answer and managed to buy myself a little more time at the expense of her peace of mind.

I was finding that I had less and less peace of mind myself now. My involvement in Marina's life was total. She was an immensely strong character and the strength which had made her a war hero sometimes made her rather imperious to live with. She had told me that she wanted a dog. She had had one as a child and she felt she would like another one now. She had spotted an advertisement in the Zagreb newspaper for a cocker spaniel puppy. Apparently it had been bought for a child in town but was proving to be too much of a handful for the family. 'Will you go and look at this dog for me?' she asked on the phone one evening when I was back in Pleso Camp. I went to look at him and he was an attractive little puppy, so I told her I thought he would be a good buy. She asked me to get him for her and she would pay me back. She insisted that she would pay for the dog as she wanted to feel he was hers from the start and not a present from me. It cost her 200 Deutschmarks, which for her at the time was over one month's pay. The dog was called Ziggy, which Marina did not like. When she had been in hospital, the first gift I took in to her was a Snoopy cartoon book, thinking I would introduce her to this character who was such a favourite in England and America.

'Oh, Snoopy!' she had exclaimed.

'You know about him?' I was surprised.

'Of course,' she said. 'When I was a student in Sarajevo everything I had was Snoopy. He was my mascot.' So she decided to change Ziggy's name to Snoopy and he went to live in Lipik.

Although electricity had been restored to the town, there was still no running water anywhere apart from the hospital, so everyone was drawing water up from wells dotted around the town. One or two children, some of them very small, started to come into the hospital with typhoid. Within a few days the number of cases had swelled to around twenty and it was obvious that somewhere in the town the disease had got into the water supply. The children who caught the disease were immediately put into ambulances and whisked away to isolation wards in Zagreb. The people became very frightened, unable to see where the disease was coming from or how to protect their children.

Marina, as the senior doctor in Lipik, set about trying to locate the cause. She had no water herself at that time and so I was still carrying over what she needed in buckets from a standpipe at the hospital and bringing drinking water up from Zagreb in a jerry-can whenever I could. She tracked the bacteria to several wells, including one just outside the block where her flat was. She closed the wells and set about treating the water supply. Thankfully the disease was halted in its tracks by her quick and positive action.

I had started to have preliminary meetings with the director of the Republic Fund in the Croatian Government and with the architect whom they had employed to do some drawings of the new building. I was very pleasantly surprised to find that they had taken this initiative because it meant that we actually had some concurrent activity going on. As the hospital was a listed building, the Government apparently needed to keep a check on what we were doing. The concept of any building having a protected status in a town which had been flattened was rather incongruous, but it seemed to be helping our cause.

'How much do you estimate the project will cost?' I asked the architect.

'About two and a half million Deutschmarks.'

I was silenced for a moment. That was about four times the rough estimate I had made while wandering around the buildings a few weeks before. 'Oh,' I said, 'okay. Well, we can do that.' So now I knew that I was looking for a million pounds. Although I was shocked by this enormous new figure I was not daunted or particularly worried. I knew we would get the money from somewhere.

Initially the director told me that whatever money I was unable to raise they would make good, which sounded fantastic. If I never raised another penny they would finish the job off for me. They obviously saw the flaw in this offer very quickly, because at the next meeting they changed their minds.

'We haven't actually got much money,' they said apologetically. 'You will understand there are many priorities for funds in Croatia at the moment. We think maybe we could donate 500,000 Deutschmarks, if you could find the rest.' This was not quite as good an offer, but I was so confident that we were going to be able to raise whatever money we needed that I did not protest. We seemed to be having so many lucky breaks, and the promises of money just kept on coming. Things seemed to be taking off on all fronts. Having swallowed my disappointment about the Bosnian job, I was enjoying my new life. I loved the feeling of having a project of my own. I was finding it very easy to break away from my old institution-alized life and I was beginning to wonder how much longer I would be able to stay in the army if this attitude continued to develop. I had enjoyed my life up till then, rarely wanting to rebel or complain, but I was tired of being a cog in a machine and I liked the feeling of being an individual.

I had to do some serious thinking about my future and whether or not I could bring myself to leave Marina. I was now approaching fifty. It would be easier for me to start a new career now than in five years' time. There was a redundancy programme in progress in the army and if you wanted to be considered for voluntary redundancy you had to submit your name by a certain date. I had been so wrapped up in everything I was doing that I had not even thought about it until now. In fact it was Caroline who brought the matter to the front of my mind when she asked, during one of our phone calls, if I was considering applying for redundancy.

'No,' I said dismissively, 'I haven't got time to think about that now I've got so much on my plate.'

'Oh, fine, that's a relief.' She was quite happy for me to stay in because she knew that they had promised to try and find me a job near home when my tour was finished in Croatia. She liked the security of army life, although she did not enjoy moving house regularly.

After I had put the telephone down I stopped to think for a moment and I wrote out a list of the advantages and disadvantages of staying in the army or going. The advantages of staying in included security and stability for another five years with the likelihood of a job at Wilton, just down the road from our home, on my return to England. At the end of five years, the children would have left university and I would have no financial responsibility for them. The disadvantages were that my chances of future promotion seemed limited – desk jobs loomed. I still had the feeling that I wanted to do something for the good of others and I felt that I was achieving that by working on the orphanage, a job I could continue if I left the army. Caroline did not want me to take redundancy, knowing that I was keen to go and do things which would take me away from home, unlike the job at Wilton. But if I did take it I could probably finish the work at the orphanage and, of course, would not be forced to make any kind of decision about my relationship with Marina.

If I went now, I would still be the right side of fifty and this would help me in getting another job. I would also get maximum compensation. I did not really know what they were going to do with me on my return home, but I did know I was unlikely to get further promotion now, particularly with the rundown of the army. I decided to opt for redundancy, but then realized that if I wanted to leave in 1993 I had about twenty-four hours to give my papers in. I immediately faxed the Ministry of Defence and asked them to add my name to the list. I had made my decision and I was pretty sure that they would select me to go. It felt as though a huge weight had been lifted off my shoulders and I was free to get on with the project which was now closest to my heart.

When I spoke to Caroline again a couple of days later I told her what I had done. She was horrified. 'But you didn't even consult me,' she protested.

'What would have been the point?' I said. 'We would only have argued, and I had made up my mind.' I then tried to convince her that my decision was sensible and that I had taken it after doing a careful appreciation of the factors, a skill we are taught in the army but which, in truth, I had rarely applied. Understandably she was very upset that I had not consulted her.

Marina had not been back to Mostar, her home town, for over a year, and had not seen her parents since they returned home from Zagreb. Mostar sounded like a very interesting place at the time, so I offered to take her down for a visit, even though the Serbs were shelling the town indiscriminately and any member of her family could have been killed at any moment. She was very excited by the prospect of seeing them and we decided to drive down from Zagreb for a long weekend. Two days before we were due to go I received a telephone call from England telling me that the Army Commander was coming out on Saturday and asking me to arrange a programme for him. I had done this tour for so many people by this stage that I was completely bored with it and decided to opt out of this one. 'I'm afraid I won't be here,' I told the caller, 'I'm going away for the weekend.'

There was a long pause. 'You can't do that,' he said

eventually, 'this is the Army Commander we're talking about.'

'Well, I'm sorry, but it's all arranged. I'll make sure there are plenty of people here to look after him.' I was rebelling for the first time in my army career, and it felt good. I couldn't have cared less about trying to impress the general. I felt liberated and confident.

When I got back from Mostar I heard that the visit appeared to have gone well. It was only much later that Caroline heard from Peter Pearson, who was the military assistant to the Commander-in-Chief, that great offence had been taken that I was not there to meet a three-star general. Apparently he had asked for an inquiry to be made as to where I was. I don't know how much they learned about what I was doing at the time, but apparently a conference was held in Wilton to decide 'what should be done with Cook'. The Serbs were shelling Mostar heavily at that time and it would have been very embarrassing for everyone if I had been injured during the weekend. I think the meeting decided that if they ignored me perhaps I would just fade away.

The Truth Comes Out

At the end of November Caroline said she would like to come to Croatia for the visit I had promised her from the beginning and to see the work that was going on at the orphanage. We would then go down to the coast for a holiday. She had become tremendously involved in the project, dealing with all the mail, faxes and phone calls which came to the house in England at all times of the day and night from around the world. Much of Caroline's life had focused on her love for children. In any other circumstances, I knew she could have been entirely involved in my work at the orphanage. I felt very mean in denying her this – it was one of the many ironies of the situation.

I wanted to show her the orphanage but, of course, I realized that it would be incredibly difficult with Marina there. Then I kidded myself that it would be all right because Caroline did not know anything about the affair and Marina promised that she would be able to behave as if nothing was wrong. In my naivety I just wanted us all to be friends. Why wouldn't they be friends, I reasoned, after all I loved them both, just in different ways?

The Macleans had offered us the use of their house on the island of Korčula, so we decided to take some time off there after Caroline had seen around Lipik. She arrived in Zagreb on a Thursday and the next day we drove out to Lipik to look at the orphanage and to meet Marina. The plan was that we would then drive Marina back to Zagreb in the evening and all go down to Selce the next day with the British soldiers, to see the children.

The moment Caroline and Marina met, I knew I had

made a terrible mistake. I could feel the friction in the air. Marina was waiting for us outside her block of flats and I walked over to her, leaving Caroline behind looking at some fruit which was for sale by the side of the road. Marina then walked off to the car in the opposite direction and we followed on, having bought some food. We met at the car and Marina had turned to ice, barely speaking to us. My driver had a picnic for us and we decided to eat it there and then in the hospital park. Snoopy was a welcome diversion and I threw bits of food for him to chase while Marina told me off. On one occasion she addressed Caroline as 'Lady Cook', but fortunately, I don't think she heard – she was wandering around with a soggy army sandwich. Disastrously, I then tried to keep conversation going while Caroline gamely joined in.

When we set off Marina sat in the front, flirting constantly with my embarrassed driver, leaning over to him, whispering and giggling while Caroline and I sat in the back of the car, trying to offset the tension by talking to Snoopy, who was jumping around from one person to another. Then he was sick, as he always was in the car. When we got back to Zagreb we dropped Marina at her aunt's flat and returned to the hotel. It was a very bad start.

Also flying out from England was a clown called Jackie who had written to me asking if he could come and entertain the children. He had already been to Romania to entertain some of the tragic orphans there and was happy to pay his own way. I had arranged for him to be flown into Sarajevo the previous day to entertain children there and then he was joining us in Selce for the weekend. We picked Marina up again in the morning and drove all the way to Selce in the same frigid atmosphere. We stopped for a picnic on the way but Marina refused to get out of the car or eat anything. We arrived at the orphanage at the same time as Jackie. He put on his show for the children, who then played games with the soldiers for the afternoon.

In the evening a dinner was arranged for the adults in the

staff room, after the children had gone to bed, with music and singing. Caroline and I were at one end of the table, while Marina sat among the soldiers at the other end and continued to flirt outrageously with them in order to punish me. Caroline was obviously feeling uncomfortable and left out, not knowing any of the people, or the words to the songs they were singing, and I felt unable to help her.

I proceeded to drink far too much and to sink into an angry melancholy. At one stage Caroline warned me that I had had too much and I flew at her furiously, telling her to mind her own business, that I would drink as much as I wanted, and she walked out of the room. After a few minutes she returned, having composed herself, and the evening carried on raucously.

Eventually I could bear it no longer and stood up, pushing my chair away. 'Good night, everybody,' I said, 'we are leaving. Thank you, Goran, thank you, everyone, for the party.' So we left and returned to our hotel in the local village. I went out on to the balcony and sat down, staring out into the night, trying to think clearly. At one stage Caroline joined me.

'What's wrong?' she asked.

'Nothing. Don't pressure me. I'll tell you some time but I can't now.'

She went unhappily back to bed. Marina and Goran, who had also driven down, were staying the night in the Selce orphanage. The next morning I decided that it would not be a good idea for us all to return in the same car, as was planned. I knew that Goran was driving back to Lipik, so I told Marina it would be better if she went with him because we were only going as far as Zagreb. He was going to leave in the morning while Caroline and I stayed down for the day with the soldiers. I could see that Marina was angry at being pushed out, but only on the following day, when I rang her, did I realize just how furious she was. I think she felt that she had lost face in the eyes of the soldiers and locals because I was there with my wife.

Coming out of St James church in Devizes, Wiltshire, on 6 May 1967 with a guard of honour of Gurkha officers

A photograph taken from a helicopter showing the three buildings, Švicarac on the left, Bellevue on the right, and the kitchen and dining room in the foreground. Švicarac was the girls' house and offices, and Bellevue was for the boys

The remains of the kitchen

One of the children's beds suspended from an internal wall

Inside one of the main buildings, showing a bath on the ground floor which had crashed down from the floor above, and twisted pipes, wires and a radiator suspended in mid-air

One Croat, one Serb and one Moslem

Marina, dressed for action during the war

Looking at plans in the ruins of the dining room with Marino the Mayor, Marina and a lady who lived next door. The clock had stuck at 5.32, which is when the first shells landed. I showed this photo to Marino on the day of the opening and he admitted to me that, at the time, he did not believe we would rebuild the home. His face shows his feelings!

With Marina and the children at Selce on the day in August 1992 that I made the
promise to rebuild their home by Christmas

Some British soldiers with Marina, Goran and a local boy, enjoying a cold drink during a well-earned break

Clearing out the rubble

Clearing the main building, Bellevue, with Sgt. Chris Biggins on the right. Bepe, one of the local men who fought bravely in the defence of Lipik, rearranged the letters of the name, and from then on it was called Djećji Dom (Children's Home) Marc Cook

The main stairway in Švicarac before and after we had removed the rubble

The visit of Sir Fitzroy Maclean, sitting, and Lady Maclean in September 1992

HRH Crown Prince Hassan Bin Talal of Jordan looking at the ruins in December 1992

Myself and Goran, taken on the last day the soldiers worked there and after we had finished clearing the buildings of rubble

Signing the building contract on 10 April 1993. Goran, myself, Marina and Mr Lojkić, the director of the building company Novogradnja. We had not raised all the money we needed at this point

Goran and Ivan Rogar outside Švicarac

Scaffolding outside Bellevue

Reconstructing the dining room

Outside my HQ at the beginning of June 1993 when Goran brought up some of the children from Selce to appear in the BBC News report

Caroline with fund-raisers from Nationwide in London, who also collected toys for the children. This was taken on 4 December 1993 and shows Dan's Van just before Caroline left in it and drove out to Lipik

Caroline on arrival at the Children's Home, having driven out from England in Dan's Van

The Dolls' House, as Švicarac was called after it was built

The two main buildings back to their former beauty, Švicarac on the left and Bellevue on the right

Caroline on the way out to Lipik in Dan's Van with a UN tanker in a ditch

Caroline near Lipik outside a ruined house once used by the Croatian army

Greeting the children as they arrived with Goran and Caroline

With the children and Dan's Van on the day they returned after they had received
their presents from Father Christmas

The roundabout, before and after. Despite being badly damaged by shrapnel, it still revolved smoothly before it was repaired

With Stanko, who has suffered so badly and needs so much love

Vladek, who captured the hearts of millions of people when he came to England and appeared on *Hearts of Gold*

Nada. Her brother ran away from another children's home about seventy miles away in the snow on Boxing Day and came to see her, arriving late at night. He was taken back by the police

Twin sisters Ivana and Romana dressed for church in Selce

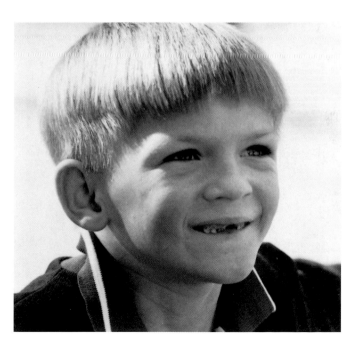

Stanko, who was the youngest child in the orphanage when it was shelled

Ivana, who arrived at the home with her young brother Sylvester, aged five, shortly after it opened. When I said to her that I was very happy that she looked after her brother so well, she replied, 'Oh, but he is all I have got'

Sylvester. While waiting for the Crown Prince of Jordan to arrive, he suddenly asked, 'Will he come on a white horse?'

Zdravko, who brought me the Christmas card. He is a lovely and sensitive boy but has many family problems, and I fear for his future

Once she had gone, Caroline had an enjoyable time playing with the children and helping Jackie the clown with face-painting. We went for a walk by the sea and I tried to tell her what was happening, but the words simply would not come. We drove back later in the day and she became more and more insistent and angry in her questioning. The following evening we went to the Esplanade Hotel to meet some media people who were out to make a film about the work of Feed the Children. One of the journalists was Charles Spencer, Princess Diana's brother, and another was a reporter from the *Daily Express* who was to play a large part in our problems later. They told us that they were going up to Lipik the following day to film.

That morning I was desperate to see Marina and try to patch things up. I left Caroline in the hotel early and went into the office. I then rang her at the hotel.

'I'm going to have to go up to Lipik for this filming. You stay in bed for a lie-in,' I said. 'I'll get back as soon as I can and we can go on to Korčula.' I hung up before she could ask me any questions. A few minutes later I got a message asking me to ring her back at the hotel.

'You're lying to me,' Caroline said. 'You don't have to go up to Lipik, why are you going?'

I could not answer her. 'Get yourself some breakfast,' I said, 'and I'll be back at lunch-time.'

I drove straight up to Lipik, where in fact the film crew never turned up. I went to see Marina, who was beside herself with anger at the way I had treated her, calling me a liar and a cheat, accusing me of stringing her along. By the time I returned to Zagreb I was in such a state of turmoil that I realized I could not go on pretending to Caroline that nothing was wrong. I had to explain what was happening to me. She was waiting anxiously in the hotel room when I got back. She had found my Croatian–English note-book which contained a list of words and phrases, some of them of a loving nature, in Marina's handwriting.

'I've got something to tell you,' I said, and proceeded to tell her the story of what had happened; that Marina could be dying and that I had made a commitment to her. Now, I explained, I loved her, and I was finding it impossible to make a decision about what to do next. 'I'm so sorry,' I ended lamely, 'but it has happened and now there is nothing I can do about it. I still love you but I am totally confused about what to do.'

Caroline's first reaction was fury against the army for sending me out to Croatia and giving me a job that left me with so much time on my hands. Then she turned on me. 'Why did you bring me out here?' she wanted to know.

'To save our marriage. Because I wanted to see you. Because you have done so much for the orphanage and I wanted you to see it. If you can try to understand and if we can talk about it, we can save our marriage.'

Although she was obviously suffering terrible hurt, she managed to remain in control after her initial burst of fury. She later told me that she suddenly realized how much she loved me and how much she too wanted to keep us together.

I tried to explain how it had happened. I felt that if we kept talking and I explained my confusion and feelings, then Caroline might understand. But of course in this first discussion, all she could really feel was anger. After a while, I said that Marina was so furious with me for bringing her out to Croatia that she wanted no more to do with me. This gave Caroline a glimmer of hope and bought us a little more time.

We went on talking for a while but then Caroline had to go to see a dentist, to keep an appointment which I had made earlier for her because of an emergency tooth problem. So, having dropped this bombshell on her, I had to take her to the dentist's surgery in Pleso Camp and leave her there to have a temporary filling. My driver waited and then brought her back to my office. That evening we were due to fly to Korčula for the holiday. By the time she arrived at the office she was subdued but fully under control. I introduced her to all the staff and then we had two hours to kill before going to the airport.

There was no privacy in the office and we could not talk freely. 'As we've got some time,' I suggested, 'do you think you could sit down and address some envelopes for me? I've written about fifty letters to companies asking for donations and I'd like to get them off before we go.'

We both needed something with which to distract ourselves and take our minds off the horrible feelings of unhappiness which we were now experiencing. So, bizarrely, within an hour of us having the most difficult conversation of our lives, Caroline had been to the dentist and now we were addressing envelopes to send letters asking for donations for the orphanage.

We got a plane to Split, stayed overnight and caught a boat over to Korčula the next day. Korčula is a delightful island, but it is a holiday resort, and by the beginning of December it was completely dead, partly because of the time of year and partly because of the war, which had emptied most of the hotels anyway. There was a feeling of sadness and desolation about the place. The Macleans' house, situated in the centre of town, next to the cathedral, was very old, with great character. It would have been the most beautiful place to be had it been a bit warmer. We talked a great deal and went for long walks. Caroline was marvellous and very loving. She kept telling me that she understood completely what had happened to me, that I had become ensnared in an emotional web because of my own softness and sentimentality. Hadn't she predicted that I would fall in love with the first pretty nurse I met in circumstances like these?

'I'm not going to just give you up without a fight, you know,' she said on one walk. 'I take my marriage vows very seriously. I love you and I'm not going to let our marriage just be blown away by one puff of wind. I was brought up to be a survivor, and you know how determined I can be when I want something. I'm a fighter and I just won't give in on this.' She was quiet for a moment. 'It'll be ironic, won't it?' she said.

'What will?'

'If you end up rebuilding the home for the children and destroying your own home in the process.'

No sooner had we arrived on the island than we got a message that the Crown Prince of Jordan wanted to visit the orphanage the following weekend. Apparently he had heard about the project from someone in England. He was going to be in the sector visiting the Jordanian troops and asked to meet me and see the project. He was such an important person that I immediately realized I must be there. By now it was Tuesday. Bad telephone lines and two language barriers led to several days of confusion and shouted phone calls, but eventually we established that he was going to be at the orphanage at nine o'clock on Sunday morning, 6 December. This was also the first anniversary of the liberation of Lipik. It was obviously going to be a big weekend in the town, with a party on Saturday night. Some of my soldiers were going up from Pleso and the children were going to be brought by bus from Selce to be lodged with families in the area, so that they could see the town for the first time since they had left more than a year before. Having lived through the bombing in the cellars and having been evacuated in closed trucks, they had never seen the full destruction which the shells had inflicted, nor the damage done by the ethnic cleansing after they escaped. I was not all that keen on them coming up until we had something better to show them, but Marina thought it would be good because of the symbolism of them returning on the anniversary date.

Caroline was obviously disappointed that our holiday was being cut short, and alarmed at the thought of returning to Lipik. However, we decided that after the weekend's celebrations we would go up to the mountains of Slovenia. We could not go to the party on the Saturday evening and so we had no idea that events would be put in motion that night which would practically destroy our fragile family life in a few months' time. It was as if someone had connected the fuse to a bomb which was now ticking away behind the scenes just waiting to explode.

When we arrived in Lipik on the Sunday morning the place was crawling with heavily armed Jordanian troops. It was wet, cold and sleeting, and I suggested to Caroline that she wait in the car rather than hang around outside getting cold and damp, even though she was very sensibly dressed in trousers and boots.

'I'll deal with the Prince as quickly as possible,' I said, 'and then I'll come back for you.'

I only waited a few minutes before the Prince arrived in his cavalcade and I started showing him around. Just at that moment Marina swept round the corner looking absolutely stunning in a full-length black fur coat thrown over her white doctor's coat and high heels, her hair flying behind her in the wind as she strode past Caroline, who was trapped behind the steamy windows of the car. Marina joined the Prince, the press and me, flashing her eyes at everybody and immediately becoming the centre of attention.

'So now you should be happy,' she said to me in an aside, 'because we are seeing the snow in Lipik together as we dreamed.'

The Crown Prince proved to be the most perfect visitor. He climbed around the rubble with me to see what we were planning and talked to the children as if he had all the time in the world. He chose to walk rather than drive to the hospital kitchen with me where we had laid on coffee. I was horribly aware that Caroline was still left in the car, all on her own, as we disappeared from sight, but I could not think of any way to go back and get her without worsening the situation for all of us. At the hospital Marina, Goran and I sat at the top table with the Prince and had our photographs taken while Caroline wandered around outside on her own. It was a hideous situation and I did not have the courage to deal with it, so I just went with the flow of events. When coffee was over we went back outside and prepared for the Prince and his entourage to depart. As he left he gave Goran a personal cheque for 10,000 dollars. When he finally drove away and we watched the cavalcade wind out behind him, Goran turned to me and said, 'The Prince visited us with his heart,' which I thought summed up this lovely man very well.

Once the Prince had gone I managed to find Caroline again. She was so angry at the way I had walked off and left her that she could hardly find the words to express herself.

We went back to Goran's flat for coffee before going up to the ruins of the local school for a celebration of the liberation of Lipik. There was a ceremony with prayers and speeches and the schoolchildren sang and danced for the assembled guests. In the row immediately in front of Caroline and me Marina was sitting with other locals. My heart sank. I asked Caroline if she would rather leave, but she bravely said she would sit it out, knowing that I was expected to be there. It was one of the longest hours of our lives.

After a big celebration lunch in the hospital the children had to start their long journey back to Selce. The British soldiers had all brought presents up from Zagreb for them. They could not communicate with one another, but they had started to form friendships. Many of the children had adopted their own individual soldiers on the first meeting and went straight back to them whenever they met, their little hands fastening on to the soldiers of their choice as soon as they spotted them. Many of the men had been going down to Selce on their own or in small groups at weekends to play football with 'their kids' and one of them, Sergeant Chris Biggins, actually left the army and went to work for Feed the Children as a direct result of his experiences in Lipik and Selce. They had raised a great deal of money back at Pleso Camp through things like a box in the bar, a raffle and an auction, and they had used some of the money to buy the Christmas presents which they had put on the seats of the bus for the journey back.

There were many tearful and emotional scenes on that cold, grey Sunday afternoon as the bus prepared to leave Lipik again. The children and Marina were crying and Caroline was obviously upset. I felt unable to comfort either of them: it was like being trapped in a nightmare. When I went into the lavatory in the hospital I found a big burly corporal sniffing noisily. 'What's wrong with you?' I asked.

'I may never see that little chap again,' he told me, his voice clogged with emotion. They were all finishing their tours and going home or on to new postings and never got to see the orphanage buildings emerge from the rubble. I hope they know that I kept my promise and their enormous efforts were not in vain.

I had originally, unrealistically, hoped that the children would be able to return home by Christmas. Instead they had had to leave Lipik once again, with their home still in ruins, and with another promise from me that I would have them back by the following Christmas.

Despite the ghastly circumstances Caroline and I had a very happy holiday together in Slovenia. It was such a relief to be with her, alone, away from the emotions of Lipik, and to be able to talk easily, and even share a joke. Communicating with Marina was always hard, not only because of the language barrier, but because of the whole cultural divide that lay between us. Neither of us ever fully understood the other, however much we may have loved one another. That made the daily task of living together both exciting and incredibly wearing. I think Caroline was able to see that part of me desperately wanted us to stay together and she felt that there was some hope if she was very careful in the way she handled me.

After the holiday we went back to Zagreb and Caroline begged me to be strong and to think of the boys and her. 'Please don't go back to her, please know that I love you.' I promised I would try to be strong, and when she had boarded the flight to London I went back to my office in an even more confused state of mind as to what I should do.

We believed that we needed to have a pool of £500,000 before we could safely ask a building company to start work, and every time someone pledged to give us some money I became wildly excited and did all sorts of mental calculations which suggested that at this rate we would have a million within months. But whenever I rang Mladen to find out exactly what had come in, the total always seemed to be a disappointment. I was beginning to learn that people do not always do as they promise, and even if they do it takes longer to organize than you first think.

I began to be able to understand much better how Marino the Mayor had felt when he first heard all my wild promises. People were continually coming to see us and promising to do all sorts of things, never to be heard from again. One weekend I was told that an American millionaire who was interested in helping us was being brought up by a minister from Zagreb. I was told he would be at the orphanage at ten o'clock on a freezing Sunday morning. So I went up to meet him and waited about two hours before he finally arrived in an official Mercedes. He was a young man called Max Primorac. I showed him around. 'I hear you've got lots of money,' I said casually.

'Well, I haven't myself,' he admitted, 'but I have contacts who have and I think this is something which they will like. There are a number of successful Croatians in America, some from orphan backgrounds.'

I went to see him in Zagreb a couple of days later with all the plans and figures and details that he needed. He seemed to me to be the perfect person to organize the American end of our fund-raising campaign. He was confident that he would be able to raise 100,000 dollars within a year.

'It would be even better if you could do it in six months,' I told him, thinking of my need to get building work started. A few weeks later, after he had returned to America, I received a letter from Paul and Stephanie Behrends, who had heard from Max and were going to set up a fund to raise the money. They also faxed through a copy of their proposed writing paper for my approval. It was headed 'The Lipik Orphanage Reconstruction Fund', with lists of smart addresses and important-looking names of people who were going to advise and preside. I was very excited. It looked as if this was a very professional outfit. As time wore on and I heard nothing I contacted them regularly and there were always endless excuses. Eventually, after many promises, they never raised a single dollar, let alone a dinar, and I had missed my opportunity to raise money in America.

Another idea I had was to write to the Sultan of Brunei, first because I had spent some time serving in his country, second because he was a Muslim, and third because he was reputed to be the richest man in the world. I rang Field Marshal Chappell, whom I knew from the Gurkhas, and asked him how to get a letter through to the Sultan.

'There are probably only two ways of doing it,' he said after a moment's thought. 'One is through Field Marshal Lord Brammell, who knows him very well, and the other is through Baroness Chalker, the Minister of Overseas Development.'

Since I had already had some luck with Baroness Chalker I thought she was my best bet. I wrote to her and she said she would be delighted to try to get a letter to the Sultan when he came over on a state visit in a few weeks' time. I wrote a letter, which I faxed to Field Marshal Chappell, who very kindly checked that I had the protocol correct, and sent it to her. Unfortunately she was unable to give it to him directly and had to pass it to a minion, at which stage I knew we had had it. If you cannot get through directly to people like this you do not stand a chance of getting past the layers of other people protecting them. I later heard that Prince Charles had written to the Sultan once and had failed to get a reply, so I knew that my chances of success were now less than nil.

Quite early on in my time in Croatia I met a charming and amusing man called Dr The Honourable Gilbert Greenall, who was working for the Overseas Development Agency, and he also accompanied us on our recce into Bosnia. He then went on to set up the European Community Humanitarian Office in Zagreb and suggested that I might have a good case for getting some money out of the EC in Brussels. I wrote a paper explaining the project, complete with costs, plans and dates, had it translated into French and sent it off to Brussels. Originally he suggested we ask for 100,000 ECUs, but when he saw the proposals he suggested increasing that to 300,000, which was about a quarter of a million pounds. I became extremely excited. Vittorio Ghide, an Italian who worked for him, came to Lipik, and I took him round the area. He borrowed a film for his camera from Marina to take lots of photographs and said it was just the sort of project he wanted to get EC funding for. We had lunch with the Mayor and he started talking about all sorts of grand projects for Lipik. None of us heard another word from him again.

For every one of these major disappointments, however, there were many other people who worked modestly, tirelessly and imaginatively to raise money for us, making no big promises and simply sending every penny they could. An enormous percentage of my time was taken up with writing thank-you letters to people who had sent individual donations of £5 or £10 which they could often ill afford, and who wanted to be kept up to date on everything that was happening. It was a time-consuming but heart-warming task. I felt strongly that £5 to these people probably meant more than £5,000 to large institutions and they must have my personal thanks. But you need a lot of £5 notes to make a million pounds and sometimes I would spend half the night writing these letters. They came to take up almost all my time and I soon realized that this was not the most professional way to raise funds. If I had spent the hundreds of hours which went into responding to small private donations pursuing large corporate and governmental donations, I would have made my own life a great deal easier. I found it impossible, however, not to respond personally to every inquiry or donation that arrived. I was exhausted as a result.

Early on in the project I received a telephone call from a New Zealand couple visiting Zagreb called Brian and Maureen Douglas, who wanted to adopt a child. They had read about us in a paper in England and wanted to meet me to see if I could help them. We spent an evening talking and I tried to find the right people for them to approach, but adopting children in Croatia is very hard and sadly for them I was unable to help. Some weeks after they returned to New Zealand, however, they wrote to thank me and asked if they could help to raise money for the orphanage. What did I need? They are both teachers, and Brian took a term off to raise money. Later two container-loads of gifts were sent all the way by sea from New Zealand via Italy to Lipik.

A Canadian girl called Suganya Lee came to visit us with her father while holidaying in Croatia and promised to help. When she got back home she organized a string of events and raised several thousand pounds for us completely on her own. Two friends in Scotland, Ros Hardie and Caro Brewster, both worked fantastically hard for us and raised many thousands of pounds with ideas like taking Smartie tubes round schools and getting the children to fill them with pound coins, and making and selling specially designed Christmas cards. Anna and David Willey in Lincoln, with their two sons Richard and Edward, wrote to Martin Bell shortly after he was injured and asked if there was anything they could do to help. He suggested that they write to me, and since contacting me they have worked every spare hour they have to raise thousands of pounds for us through hundreds of small donations. Every week I seemed to be receiving more money from them.

The Willey family threw a garden party at their home to which they invited Martin Bell and me. I was in England at the time and was keen to go. It was the first time I had seen

Martin since his injury. The Willeys' small and immaculate garden was absolutely packed with stands and stalls, all of which were pulling in money for us. Martin also put a number of people our way, including his sister, who breeds Birman cats in Cambridge and asked anyone who bought kittens to send the money to us. I had no idea that pedigree cats fetched such exorbitant prices! My old regiment, the 10th Gurkha Rifles, raised £1,000 for us when my friend Peter Pearson, who was now in command, sent out the Pipes and Drums to play at an engagement in Hong Kong. Fiona Sparrow, the wife of the British Ambassador in Zagreb, gave her mother a Christmas present of some money, but told her it was for Lipik, not for her. There have been so many people who have worked unbelievably hard for us and have been such a help that I wish I could mention them all personally, but it would double the length of this book. I hope they all know how grateful we were and continue to be for their efforts and I have included a list of them at the end of the book.

At the end of December my tour of duty as COMBRIT-CON was officially over and I was due to go back to England. I was in no hurry to depart and I thought that if I just kept quiet they would leave me where I was for a few more months until my redundancy came through. I was now so emotionally involved with Lipik, Marina and the children that I did not know what to do. I could not bear the thought of Caroline and Edward being on their own for Christmas, with both Will and me away, and I managed to indulge on a flight back to England for the holiday ('indulging' means getting a free flight on a Forces plane which is flying the route anyway), and returned a week later.

Marina was upset that I was not staying for Christmas with her, but she went to her aunt in Zagreb and was pleased that I was returning in the New Year. Her health had improved a great deal with the treatment. The cool of the winter helped her skin, although she still had some angry red patches. Most of the time her energy levels were high again, although she would occasionally be overcome by weariness. She was now becoming active in local politics, on top of her work at the hospital. They were holding the first local elections since independence and Marina was persuaded to stand. That meant that our evenings were often spent going to meetings so that she could talk from the hustings, canvassing for her party, the HDZ Party. She is a popular local figure, highly respected for her professional status as a doctor and for her forceful and dynamic personality. To the local community, many of whom are simple farming people, she is an impressive and sophisticated lady. She is known for being able to use her tongue like a whiplash, so people always know where they stand and are wary of crossing her. She had also earned her street credibility by fighting in the war. Despite her youth and her gender, she could more than hold her own in the male-dominated world of Croatian local politics. She was a powerful, emotional speaker and she had little trouble in winning enough votes to get into office, representing Lipik at County Council level. I told Caroline how busy Marina was and how that meant that we did not get to see much of each other any more, and that her parents had given her a talking-to, pointing out the error of her ways. I think Caroline felt there was some hope for her in this, but my few days in England were tense and unhappy none the less.

I managed to spin out my departure date to mid-February as the medical colonel who was going to take over from me as COMBRITCON was due to go on leave for a few weeks. I was very lucky also that a UN civilian called Alistair Livingstone was posted to my camp headquarters as my opposite number responsible for administration. He had spent many years in the British army and the US Marines and was extremely energetic and efficient. He was keen to get on with his new job, and I was delighted to let him do mine as well, which allowed me more time to concentrate on Lipik. Fortunately Alistair and I hit it off from the start, and he quickly became a good and very understanding friend.

When I left England for Zagreb after the five-day Christmas break, I managed to convince Caroline that I would not be seeing Marina any more, that I would be home in February and it would all be over. Eventually I had to admit that I would have to go up to Lipik for a week before leaving the country to finalize a few things at the site. At this news Caroline announced that she could not stand the thought of sitting around in England imagining what was happening, and she was going to take herself off on holiday. She booked into a chalet skiing holiday in France and did not tell me where she was going.

In February I could not put my departure off any longer and I returned to England and Caroline. Once home, I was able to devote myself full-time to raising more money and chasing sums that had already been promised. I felt that I was hanging in a sort of limbo between my past and my future. I could not see clearly what was going to happen, so I concentrated on one day at a time, but I was missing my life in Lipik terribly.

13

When One Door Opens

In the middle of March I was heading back to Lipik to decide who would be awarded the building contract. I now thought we had just about enough money to make this commitment and I imagined that if we got something happening more money would start rolling in again. Since I had returned to Britain everything seemed to have ground to a halt on the project. The soldiers had gone home and the site was once more standing silent and desolate. The shells of the buildings might have been cleared but the rubble was still there, in heaps outside the windows, waiting to be taken away. Birds were nesting in cracks and crevices of the remaining walls and there seemed no reason why things should ever change. There was nothing going on to catch people's imagination and, as a result, the flow of money had slowed down. I believed that I needed to be there to make sure things kept happening or the children would still not be home by the end of 1993.

If I could get the building work started, people would be able to see that it was an on-going project and would feel more inclined to help. I flew back and attended a number of Government meetings with Miss Kaya Bakalic, the very helpful new director of the Republic Fund. They had advertised for building companies to put in their tenders for the job, and had had six bids which we opened a few days before Easter. Three were from big Zagreb building companies and three were from around Lipik. I was very surprised to find that companies were still operating in the area.

All the quotes were in the region of a million pounds, as the architect had predicted, although one bid was considerably less and the builder was offering a package with all sorts of extras, including a personal donation if he got the contract. We were about to give it to him when the director got cold feet and went to see the minister, who warned that this might not be the best company to go to. An independent firm called Interkonzalting had been appointed to oversee the whole contract and the construction process, and they advised us to go for one of the other local companies. In the end we selected Novogradna in the nearby town of Daruvar.

During these interminable meetings in Government offices I had trouble keeping my mind on the business in hand as I struggled with my emotional problems. Whenever I went home to Lipik Marina would tell me that I had to make up my mind and choose, and whenever I spoke to Caroline on the phone I heard the same thing, with her begging me to be sensible and think what I was doing. I knew they were both right, but I could not bear the thought of giving up either of them. I was again very confused and I thought that God must be too. Caroline, I knew, walked regularly across the water-meadows to the tiny church at Little Langford and asked for His help, and Marina prayed daily to 'her' Jesus. I felt like piggy in the middle.

I had a return ticket to England on the Thursday before Easter. A few days before Marina and I had a very stormy day when she basically told me to make up my mind or go, so I theatrically ripped up my return ticket and promised to ring Caroline and tell her that I was leaving her and not going back. I just could not bring myself to leave Lipik again and return to the life I was leading in Wiltshire, pretending to be part of a community when my heart was so far away. The time had come to make a choice between my old and my new life. I knew now that however much I wanted to keep both, it was not possible. By dithering I was hurting both Caroline and Marina and I could not get away with it any longer.

The tension between Caroline and me in England had been terrible and I had been behaving very oddly, withdrawing in order to avoid being questioned about anything and becoming angry when she persisted. There had been a number of painful discoveries like a Valentine card, letters and faxes from Marina. Each discovery led to angry accusations from Caroline and feeble excuses from me as I struggled to survive from day to day. Funnily enough, we seemed to get on better over the telephone than we did when we were together. I picked up the phone and dialled with a terrible feeling of dread.

It took many attempts before I got a connection. I rang our great friend Bill Dawson first and explained what I was going to do and asked him to drive to our home to be with Caroline when I broke the news to her. As always, the Dawsons were very kind, gentle and understanding, and Bill agreed immediately to go. Every time I dialled Caroline's number I hoped I would not be able to get through, but eventually I did.

It was a desperately hard call and a cowardly thing for me to have done, something I am not at all proud of. Caroline told me that she understood how I felt and she believed it was something that I had to get out of my system. She still believed that if she made me make a final choice there and then I would have been unable to give up my new life in Lipik, but that if she waited patiently I might one day return to her. It was the most extraordinarily brave and intelligent way to handle an impossibly hurtful situation. I did not deserve such considerate treatment and I was deeply grateful to her for not washing her hands of me. She had allowed me, once again, to put off my final decision, strongly believing that if she waited for the right moment I would decide to return home to England.

'The door here will always be open to you,' she told me. 'One day, hopefully, you will come back through it.'

I was amazed by her strength and wisdom and wondered how many other wives would have said that. Had she said then, 'Get out, I never want to see you again,' I suppose I would have had no alternative but to throw myself completely into my new life. Knowing that the door was always open at home meant that I never really totally committed myself to Marina. It is clear to me now that it would have been very much more difficult to have raised all the money had I stayed in Croatia, and many of the events which were to follow and which ended in the successful completion of the project were a direct result of Caroline's incredible understanding and fortitude.

That evening Marina and I walked out into the grounds of the orphanage and sat on a bench overlooking what had once been the children's playground. The ground was pockmarked with craters from the shells, the bench broken, gnarled and splintered. As we sat looking out over the devastatation at the lifeless, ruined houses and damaged trees beyond, I told her that I would not be going back to England, that I had finally made my choice and that I would be staying with her for good. I felt elated, telling myself that I had finally had the courage to make up my mind, but disgusted at myself for the way I had treated Caroline. I felt excited and confident about the coming months and horribly frightened that I might come to regret what I had done.

On Easter Sunday Marina and I went for coffee with Goran and Gordana at their flat. As we were talking the phone rang and Goran answered it. 'Yes, yes, he is here. Mark,' he called to me, 'it is for you.'

I went out into the hall and picked up the receiver, knowing who it was.

'Hallo, it's me.'

'Hallo, how are you?' I responded feebly.

'How do you think I am? Bloody miserable.'

She had been invited out to lunch with friends but did not want to go, she felt too low to be good company to anyone. I felt desperately sorry for her, and guilty. When we finished talking I could not face going back to the others so I went outside into the garden and wandered about. They could see me from the windows and knew that I was unhappy. When we left, Marina asked me who was on the phone.

'It was Caroline.'

'It is good that you are telling me the truth at last. I knew it was her but I wanted to see if you would lie to me. How do you think it makes me feel knowing that you want to be in England with your family and not here with me? It makes me angry. Why do you want to make my life so hard and embarrass me in front of people?'

I tried to explain how I felt, but it was impossible. I could see why she would be feeling hurt, we were all hurting.

Back in England, Edward persuaded Caroline to go out and get herself two part-time jobs, one in a nursery school and the other as a matron in a prep school in Salisbury. I think they were a great help to her. Apart from Edward, Caroline had no close family in England. Her only other relative was her brother, a bachelor farmer out in South Africa. She wrote telling him that I had left her and some weeks later received a postcard in response. 'How's the cruel world treating you?' it read. 'Remember to send the boys up ladders regularly to keep the gutters clean.'

During the run-up to the building contract being awarded we had a number of meetings with the Croatian Government which seemed to go on for ever, until I wanted to scream with frustration. One in particular seemed to be everlasting and I finally could not stand it any longer.

'Look,' I said, 'I have a ticket to go back to England in two days' time. If we don't reach an agreement now I am going to withdraw the British support and find something else to do with the money. There is a project very like this which badly needs help in Belgrade.' There was a hushed silence and then the director of the Republic Fund asked if I would mind waiting a moment while she went to speak to her minister. Obviously the thought of losing such aid to the Serbs was more than they could stand. All the problems which had apparently been holding us up were suddenly resolved and they agreed to find half the money needed for the project. I had raised about £200,000 at that stage and I was confident that we could find another £300,000 by the time the builder needed to be paid the next instalment.

This was not the first time the bureaucrats had made us angry. At one stage, when we were already well into the project, some men turned up at the site and unfurled a new set of plans. Marina knew them as men from the local council. When we looked at the drawings we saw that they had decided to turn the park and Kursalon complex into a tourist attraction. The area where the orphanage stood was designated to be a car park and information centre.

We were horrified. 'But what about the children's home?' I asked.

'Oh, there is good news on that,' they told us. 'There is a piece of land next to the school building at the top of the town. It is the perfect place for a children's home and it will cost us much less to build it from scratch there than to rebuild here.'

I was speechless but Marina was ferocious. Our dream did not involve a cheap, pre-fabricated concrete building going up on a disused lot at the back of town. We wanted to return the original, hundred-year-old building to its former glory. For the first time I realized just how powerful Marina was among the political figures of the area. She started to make telephone calls, pulling strings and gaining support. Then she set about the people who were trying to betray our plan and refused to brook any arguments. She threatened to lose people their jobs by talking to friends in high places if this new plan was not scrapped immediately. Goran and I were due to go down to Zagreb the next day for meetings and she told them that the plans which we had originally discussed must be agreed by seven in the morning for us to take with us, otherwise heads would roll. Sure enough, when Goran went to the office at seven the next morning, a letter of authorization was waiting for him, just as she had instructed.

At another meeting officials told me it had been decided that the project was going to be too expensive and it would be better to pull down the buildings and put up a custom-made modern structure for the children somewhere else. I was furious and stormed down to Zagreb for a meeting with more senior people. Unfortunately Marina was not available to come with me and so I took a professional interpreter, a very strong woman who worked for me in Pleso Camp. I couldn't believe my ears when, halfway through the meeting, she started to agree with the officials as well.

'I think this does sound like the best plan,' she told me. 'I think we should agree to it.'

'Would you mind sticking to translating,' I snapped back furiously, frustrated by my own helplessness against the language barrier and beginning to wonder how accurate she was actually being in her interpretation of my words. Fortunately they thought better of their alternative scheme and we were soon back on course.

Another alternative suggested, when the money seemed to be coming in too slowly for comfort, was to restore one building at a time. I hated this idea because I could see that that way the project would drag on for years, until everyone was bored with hearing about it. Worst of all, however, it would mean that the children would have to live on a building site if they moved into the first building when it was completed. Not only would that be unpleasant for them, it would be downright dangerous. So I insisted that all three buildings must go up at once as planned.

On 10 April 1993, in the ruins of the orphanage, we signed the contract for the building work to commence immediately and to be completed in five months or 150 working days. I prepared to establish myself full-time on the site. A friend of ours, who ran the mineral water factory on the outskirts of Lipik, lent us a caravan which I had towed into the park just behind the site, among the trees, away from where the worst of the dust was likely to be. This was to be my headquarters.

The local authorities came and fixed me up with an electricity line, telephone and fax machine, and I was fully operational as the spring leaves began to unfurl around me. The caravan had a bright orange camping awning attached to the outside and I managed to salvage some white plastic furniture from the burnt-out restaurant in the destroyed swimming-pool complex on the other side of the park. Everything had bullet and shrapnel holes in it but I found half a dozen chairs and a couple of tables that were not too badly damaged, and cleaned them up and put them outside under the awning. Somebody gave me an umbrella and stand and I made a barbecue out of old bricks and metal, using logs collected in the park as fuel. There was a fridge in the caravan for drinks.

The locals had been doing a lot of work in the park in the previous few months, clearing the fallen trees and undergrowth. The damage inflicted by the shells was still obvious among the broken tree-tops, but at ground level the spring flowers were able to break through among the tree-trunks.

On the following Monday morning I was very excited and waited for the expected army of builders to arrive. I wandered around all day, occasionally making telephone calls and being assured that everything was under way. By the time darkness fell and nothing had happened I was concerned. The next morning I went down again and found one small cement mixer standing next to the ruins. This was impossible! They would never make it by Christmas at this rate. But over the course of the next few days the most enormous vehicles started to roll into town, bringing a giant remote-controlled crane and every imaginable piece of building equipment. To me it all looked like a good, professional military operation.

In the first few weeks it was all destruction, with everything that had to be demolished, like the old chimneys, internal walls and the porch which we were replacing with a big conservatory-style entrance, crashing to the ground in clouds of dust. Then a relative calm settled over us and the artisans arrived. Rows of carpenters who would be making all the window-frames and internal woodwork set up their benches among the craters on the playing field. Neat piles of materials appeared everywhere on the site. In my ignorance I had imagined that they would start by putting on the roof, to keep everything dry, and then work underneath it. Of course they left the roof to last so that they could lower things in and out by crane. The whole project was supervised by Ivan Rogar, the quantity surveyor from Interkonzalting, who used to drive up each day from Zagreb in his little red Renault and check that everything was going to plan and specification. Ivan must have saved us tens of thousands of pounds with his vigilance.

My job was to continue to keep the money coming in by raising awareness of the project around the world. Goran was also linked up to a fax at his home, a surprisingly sophisticated development considering that they still had no running water in the flat. He was busy organizing things like the teachers and equipment in preparation for the children's eventual return. He also handled the money between SOS for Children and the builders, thereby ensuring that it did not get delayed or lost while passing through the hands of middlemen.

The builders would arrive at 7 a.m. and I would go round the site checking on progress. Every morning I would go to my caravan headquarters and write begging letters and send faxes. One brief telephone call could often take an hour to make as lines were very erratic. What should have been quick communications were often major operations, which was very frustrating and a complete contrast to my army experience and ordinary life in Britain. Every time it rained, the telephone lines stopped working. Another frustration was the sporadic appearance of incoming mail – a letter took eight days to come from England, which meant that I used the fax machine more than normal and so doubly depended on the vagaries of the telephone lines. The orphanage was a big project, not something to run out of a caravan with one fax machine that might or might not work. Sending a single-page fax was a major achievement. All the letters and faxes were handwritten, and then they had to be filed. Goran and I spent about two days a week in Zagreb for meetings with Government officials, aid organizations and architects. Even a simple meeting meant being out of the caravan office for a whole day.

To show us all, and any visitors or media, where we were getting to with the fund-raising, I prepared one of those thermometer charts which fund-raisers all over the world love so much. On the left-hand side of the thermometer I had a dozen or so yellow stickers with the names of organizations who had pledged to raise money. My hope was that these stickers would move on to the thermometer itself when the money actually came in. Very few of those organizations, I am afraid, actually came up with the money they had promised.

Marina was now the permanent local doctor, working in her 'Ambulance', as they called the GP surgery, just across the park. As she was one of the few people in Lipik who could speak any English she played a major role in talking to the many delegations of people who came to visit us during this period. She was also busy with her politics and receiving any aid that reached the town, signing for it to ensure that it did not find its way on to the black market.

A few weeks later we were ready for the laying of the foundation stone, which was due to be a big day, complete with visiting dignitaries and speeches. The television cameras were there to film the director from Zagreb and me shovelling in the cement. During the normal speeches the only words I understood were a reference to me as a '*brzo, brzo*' person, a 'quickly, quickly' man. Everyone laughed as apparently I had acquired a reputation for pressurizing Government authorities and always demanding things immediately.

Just as I was about to put in the first shovelful of cement someone ran up with two spotlessly shiny, white hard hats for the director and me to wear. The moment the ceremony was over the helmets were whipped away and I never saw another one worn on the site from that day to the day of completion. Nor did I see the foundation stone again. It was quite literally a foundation stone, being buried under the entrance, complete with my name and the date on it. Maybe it will be unearthed in another hundred years. I hope not.

The builders always started work early in the morning and finished by around four o'clock, leaving us to sit tranquilly outside the caravan in the park, listening to the birdsong which had been drowned out by the sounds of building work all day, and viewing the work in progress as the sun set behind the playing fields, bathing the growing building in a warm pink light.

We had many visitors coming to see us at the caravan – the media, Government officials, representatives of aid organizations and well-wishers from all over the world – and I realized I needed a sign to show them where to find the caravan. I decided to make Snoopy into our emblem and asked the builder to create some signs with Snoopy on them, directing people to the caravan, with 'My HQ' at the entrance to the site and 'Snoopy HQ, Please Do Not Disturb' outside my caravan.

This attracted a lot of attention, all of which helped to raise awareness of what we were doing and give it an appropriately childish theme. Marina became quite upset that Snoopy, who was 'her dog', was being adopted so completely by the project, but he had endeared himself to too many people by then to withdraw from public life. As a puppy he had gone down with us to meet the children in Selce, who had been absolutely delighted with him, almost pulling him to pieces in their enthusiasm, endlessly throwing things for him to chase, or trying to cuddle him as he licked their faces and simultaneously struggled to be free of their loving embraces.

He spent most of his days in the park with me, and was spoilt by everyone who came near. He also appeared on Croatian television several times. On one memorable occasion he chewed through his lead while sitting with Marina in the audience of a chat show on which I was appearing. Finally breaking loose as the show was being broadcast, he hurtled across the studio floor and landed in my lap while I was being interviewed, leaping and bounding all over me and licking my face. This surprise appearance delighted viewers, including his previous owners, who had been watching the show at home and called to say how pleased they were to see him looking so well, and several other people who rang in accusing us of stealing their dogs.

One of the great spin-offs of the project, which I had not anticipated, was that by using local labour and materials we were actually bringing work and money into the area, helping the local economy to start up again. Quite soon after work began on site, some men started to repair one of the houses in the street opposite. The owners of this house also owned a successful bar in Pakrac called Number One and they intended to turn this building into Number Two, providing meals as well as drinks. It was an enterprising idea since the only place in Lipik for anyone to go at that stage was Jura's café, where they did not serve food, and we all started to frequent Number Two regularly. In one room was a bar, with a few extra stools and corner shelves, and through the arch there were three or four tables where people could choose from a menu of several kinds of meat and chips. Although the ingredients became monotonous if you ate there too often, the food was fresh and the helpings generous.

Number Two was soon as popular as Jura's café in the evenings, full of local families who had returned to the town but grown tired of the struggle to cook for themselves in what was left of their homes, using ingredients which mostly had to come from the aid convoys. By the end of an evening the cigarette smoke would be so thick in the air you could hardly see across the room and there were nearly always two or three men who were rather drunk. Drink is a problem in the area, simply because there is little else for people to do and because it helps them to forget everything that has happened and is still happening in their lives. Whenever Marina and I went in there she would usually end up with people standing, sitting and kneeling around her as she held court. I became entranced by these tough people who seemed able to laugh and cry almost simultaneously, always eager to buy us drinks and tell us their woes. I kept wishing that I could master their language, but despite taking lessons, I still found it extremely difficult.

In May my son Edward came out to visit us for a week, which made me very happy indeed but hurt Caroline greatly. He stayed with us at Marina's flat and came to work with me in the caravan each morning. At the weekend we all drove down to Selce to visit the children. Marina often talked to them in intense little huddles and on that weekend I saw her deep in conversation with Drajen, a particularly naughty thirteen-year-old boy. She later told me about their conversation.

'I think Edward is very proud,' Drajen told her.

'Why shouldn't he be?' Marina wanted to know. 'He's a fine young man. He has much to be proud of.'

'He is proud,' Drajen said gravely, 'because Mark chose him and made him his son. If that hadn't happened he would be just like us.'

Caroline and I still remained in almost daily contact over the telephone and she took considerable heart from the tales Edward told on his return to England about how volatile my relationship with Marina was. I was very tempted to get on the plane back with him but I knew that the time was not yet right. Our wedding anniversary was on the very day of his return to England and I'm afraid that all I gave him to take back was a very inadequate note for Caroline.

14

Attacked by the Gutter Press

Several television crews visited us over the next three months, including George Eykyn, a reporter from BBC Breakfast News, who had done a story on us right at the beginning and came back to see how we were progressing. He arrived in June and wanted to set up a scene with some of the children from Selce coming back to see how their home was progressing. Goran drove down to Selce to fetch five of the children and we met them, with the cameras, coming back into the protected area at the UN checkpoint. We then filmed them arriving at the orphanage, being greeted by me and being shown the reconstruction.

The boys went up in the crane to look down on the walls rising up from below, and then they all went down into the cellars to show the cameras how it had been during the bombings. At that stage we had not got round to clearing them out and all the old mattresses and comics were still lying around. The British soldiers had previously cleaned out some of the nastier things, such as some very unpleasant vats of stew and soup and trays of old eggs, which had been standing around for a year by then and nearly made even these experienced medics throw up. Bryan Sparrow, the ambassador, also came up, with his wife, to spend the day with us and be interviewed.

The next night I had a dream that Marino the Mayor had called me into his office and told me that the people of Lipik were upset that I was living with their doctor. He asked me to move out and live somewhere else.

The film was due to be shown in Britain the following Wednesday morning. On Tuesday Marina and I went out in the cool of the evening for a walk with Snoopy. We crossed the railway line into a little village on the other side, strolling through the ruined houses to a UN checkpoint. Marina wanted to visit a dog which some Canadian soldiers had brought in to her for repairs to a badly lacerated leg a few days before. I was there at the time when they ran in shouting, 'Is this the vet's?'

'No,' I laughed, 'this is actually the doctor's.' At that moment Marina had come out of her office and agreed to bandage the animal up.

On this evening the Canadian platoon commander invited us in for a cup of coffee and we chatted for a while and saw that the dog was okay, before wandering back through the ruins to Marina's block. A number of children were playing on the front steps, and with them was Marino the Mayor. We told him of my dream the night before and he was highly amused, his eyes twinkling as he laughed. He thought it very funny that I should have had such a dream and he assured me that he was very happy for me to live with Marina.

The truth was that their lives had been so totally changed by the war that their values of what was right and wrong and what was important had been put under extreme pressure. There had been several broken marriages in Lipik as a result.

Marino's four-year-old daughter, Nikolina, followed us into the flat.

As we came in the telephone rang and Marina picked it up. Nikolina was bouncing round the room with Snoopy. She was making a lot of noise and I was playing with them, only half hearing what Marina was saying in the background. I realized she was talking in English and gradually more and more phrases began to get through to me over the barking and squealing.

'Yes, he's here if you want to speak to him ... Yes, it's fantastic, he's done a wonderful job ... we're so lucky, it's all going very well ... Yes, I have cancer but it is under control, I continue with my life ... Yes, very lucky that he helped me

. . . Yes, he's staying here at the moment, I have many people staying in my flat because there are no hotels here in Lipik now . . . that's right, no, but he's here . . .' The conversation seemed to go on and on and I began to be curious as to who she was talking to. Eventually she said, 'Okay, I'll hand you over to him,' and she handed me the phone with a disinterested shrug.

Puzzled, I took it from her. 'Hallo, this is Mark Cook speaking.'

'Hallo, Colonel Cook, this is Annie Leask from the *Daily Express*, we have actually met before, although you may not remember, you were with your wife at the Esplanade Hotel in Zagreb.'

I had a vague memory of going to the Esplanade Hotel to meet some reporters with Caroline when she was out in December. They were all out with Anglia Television to do a story about Alan Waller's Feed the Children operation and he had suggested we drop in for dinner. One of the reporters was Annie Leask, but she had not made any particular impact on us at the time.

'Oh yes,' I said noncommittally, 'how are you?'

'I just had a nice long chat with Dr Topić and I gather you are living with her there.'

'Yes, but Dr Topić has many people staying with her here. There are very few places to stay in Lipik.'

'I gather it is just a one-bedroom flat.'

'That's right, but . . .'

'Does your wife know that you are there?'

'Yes, she does. In fact my son has been out to visit us.'

'What does she think about it?'

'I don't know, you had better ask her.' I was not handling it well but she had caught me completely unawares: one minute I had been playing with a dog and a child and suddenly I was being grilled about my private life.

'Is this her telephone number?' She read off our number at home.

When I finally came off the phone I was shaking. Marina was completely bemused, she had no idea of the significance of what had just happened. People in Croatia have no concept of a tabloid press and she could see no reason why any newspaper would want to publish details of our private lives. I tried to explain that this was not actually good news, that it was a very serious situation. Not only did Marina not understand about British newspapers, she could also not understand why I would be embarrassed to talk to anyone about our relationship. 'You say you love me,' she said challengingly. 'Why do you want to hide it from people? Are you ashamed of me?'

'I've got to ring Caroline and warn her,' I said. I dialled our home number but it was too late, the line was engaged. I gave up and tried to explain the situation to Marina again. As I talked the phone rang and Marina answered it.

'May I speak to Mark Cook, please?' the voice said.

'Who's calling?' Marina asked.

'It's his mother.'

'I think it is your wife.' Marina handed me the phone.

'I've just had the *Daily Express* on.' Caroline sounded furious. 'Why the hell didn't you warn me they were going to call? What's going on?'

I realized that I had handled it all completely wrong. 'Just give me a few minutes to think,' I said, 'and I'll ring you back.'

'I've got to go to the caravan and make some calls,' I told Marina, and went out into the night. As soon as I got to the caravan I rang Caroline. 'What did you tell her?' I asked.

'What could I say? I told her the truth. I said, yes, I did know what was going on. No, I was not very happy about it. I told her you were caught in a web, that the project meant so much to you and that I was going to hang on because one day I hoped you would come back. She says there is going to be something about it in the papers tomorrow.'

We talked for a long time and then I rang George Eykyn,

as his film about the orphanage was due to be shown in a few hours' time. I thought it was only fair, as he had been so good to me, to warn him that this was about to happen.

'George,' I said when I got through to him, 'I've got very bad news. The *Daily Express* has been on to us and they are planning to do a story about Marina and me and my marriage to Caroline.' George had been vaguely aware of the situation but had not been interested in my private life as far as his story went. He wanted to cover the restoration of the building and the visit of the children. He couldn't have cared less about my personal problems professionally, even though he had been very considerate towards me personally. While he was with us he had tried to get an interview with Marina after filming Bryan Sparrow and me and the children, but by that time Marina's nose had been put so far out of joint by the attention everyone else was getting that she had refused to talk to him. She was beginning to believe that she did not exist as far as the British media were concerned and that they were only interested in my role. To a degree her complaints were justified, but then, as I tried to explain to her, every national media tends to be parochial and write mainly about its own people.

'I don't think my boss will be put off running the story tomorrow morning, because it's a good piece,' George said when I had told him the whole story, 'but I must tell him what's happening. Thank you for letting me know. I'll call you back.'

I waited at the caravan, knocking back the odd whisky or two, until George rang back. 'No, it's okay,' he said, 'my boss says we'll still run the story and to hell with what the *Daily Express* print.'

I stayed at the caravan, thinking and drinking and wondering what on earth I was going to do. At about midnight the fax machine started to work. A broadsheet came through from George with a message scrawled across it: 'BAD NEWS! The following is a copy of front page of *Express*!' I stood there with bated breath as the machine whirred and chuntered and slowly forced out a two-inch-high, thick black banner headline:

WAR HERO NUMBER TWO IN LOVE SPLIT

The story filled virtually the whole of the front page of the paper. I could not believe that for a major newspaper the most important piece of news in the world that day was my relationship with a Croatian doctor. What possible relevance or importance did it have to anyone apart from my family? I understood that the media's appetite had been whetted by Lieutenant Colonel Bob Stewart, who was the 'War Hero Number One' they were alluding to. Apparently he had met an aid worker in Bosnia and stories had appeared in some newspapers, but as I had not been in England at the time I had not read any of the coverage. All too many people get divorced and have troubles in their marriages, so why would the public be interested in a couple of old soldiers? This was my first experience of the tabloid press and I was horrified by what I read and terrified that it might endanger the project on top of the hurt it would inflict on Caroline and the boys. Beneath the headline were pictures of the three of us, 'the Colonel, his wife and his lover'.

I rang Caroline and told her that it was far worse than we had expected. I suggested that she leave the house and go to stay with friends before other media picked up the story and came down to Wiltshire.

'No.' She was adamant. 'I'm not going to be driven out of my home by these people.'

'Well, I'm coming back.'

'It would be lovely to see you, but don't feel you have to come because of this.'

In the morning I went back to the flat and showed the newspaper to Marina. She was completely perplexed, and incensed at being described as 'his lover'. It was a horrible word and seemed to cheapen our whole relationship. For me it had been one of the most profound emotional experiences of my life, as I believe it was for Marina. She often told me that the moment she saw me from the balcony above the Nepalese soldiers, she had felt that she would be willing to go with me anywhere in the world, right there and then, without knowing any more about me. It was the most consuming relationship from the first moment, and neither of us could bear to see it summed up in that one trite word, 'lover'.

'I'm sorry,' I said, 'but I am going to have to go back to England. My family is going to be besieged by the media after this.'

I had been waiting for something to happen that would make up my mind for me. I knew that I was not strong enough to make the choice for myself: I needed some outside force to make the decision for me and this seemed to be it. I had been becoming more and more fatalistic in recent months. Often, when I had been driving like a maniac between Zagreb and Lipik, I had thought that if I had an accident and was killed that would solve all my problems: the choice would be out of my hands, no more decisions to make. So now things *were* out of my hands and I could respond to the call of duty, something I was more familiar and comfortable with than any of the emotions I had been experiencing.

Marina watched as I packed up my things in the flat and then we went over to the caravan to collect up my belongings from there. She was very distressed. She was due to go into Kutina for an appointment with her specialist that morning and when she returned she brought me some small farewell presents. She went on duty at the hospital that afternoon.

'I'll come and see you before I go,' I promised. 'Ivan Rogar is going back to Zagreb, he'll give me a lift.'

Caroline rang to tell me that she had been shown the story by the general's wife who lived across the road, who had come down early in the morning, the moment she saw the papers, to see if there was anything she could do to help.

'The general's wife reads the *Daily Express*?' I was surprised.

'She says she never normally does, but her sister happens to be staying, and she likes it,' Caroline explained. 'Anyway, it was kind of her to call.' I told her that I would be back the next day and she said she would meet me at the airport.

For the last ten years I have had a personal rule about never drinking alcohol before six in the evening. That day I broke it. It was very hot and I went across to Number Two with Ivan and Goran. We sat under an umbrella and drank beer. Marino the Mayor came by to chat, and then Jura and other locals, whom I had got to know, joined us. I decided that I could not just disappear without telling these men what had happened. I had promised Marina that I would not tell anyone but I had had a few beers by now and I felt they ought to know so that they could protect her if anything happened after I had gone.

'Look,' I said, 'I have to tell you what has happened.' Ivan translated for me. I showed them the newspaper and they simply could not believe their eyes. 'Please look after Marina,' I said, 'because she is going to get very upset and I don't think I will be able to come back to Lipik.'

'You are saying goodbye to us for ever?' All of them were staring at me now.

'Yes, I think I am.'

'But the project is only half done,' Goran protested.

I promised them all that I would continue to raise money for the home and do anything I could for Lipik from England.

There was nothing else I could say and I could not speak without the tears coming. We had a few more beers until it was time for me to go. Ivan drove me round in his little Renault Four to say goodbye to Marina. Fortunately there were no patients there at the time, only her kind nurse, Ankiza, who had become a good friend to both of us. Marina was very calm and she admitted that she had taken a sedative. I told her quickly that she was a very special girl and she would soon find a Croatian man of her own age. Then I left and we set off into the sunset, bouncing through the potholes, leaving Marina and Snoopy and Lipik behind.

15

Torn between Two Places

It was a relief to get back to England and see Caroline's face waiting for me at the airport. I felt so bad. I knew that what I had been doing was wrong and my conscience was like a lead weight. I knew that I still loved Marina as well as Caroline, and I also loved my family and my home. Now I had succeeded in hurting everyone and turning our lives into a sordid media circus.

We stopped on the way home to collect Jess, our golden retriever, from Bill and Kay Dawson and to have tea with them before getting back into the car for the last half-hour's journey home. Both Caroline and I were extremely lucky with our friends. One of the good aspects of army life and moving about as much as we had was that we had made many good friends with whom we kept in touch and who were aware of our problems. All these, without exception, refused to take sides. All of them wanted to do anything they could to help us both through this very difficult time in our lives. Many of them were an enormous source of support to Caroline when I was being no support to her at all, and none of them turned their backs on me or chastised me for what I had done.

We had been driving for about five minutes when a car came roaring up behind us with its lights flashing. I realized it was Bill Dawson, whose house we had just left. I pulled over and got out to see what he wanted. 'I've just had a call from your neighbours,' he said, 'to say that the press are picketing your house. They think that if you go round the back you will be able to get in across the fields without being noticed. They thought you might like to know before you arrived.'

'What do you think?' I said to Caroline. 'Shall we go round the back way and sneak in?'

'They won't go away,' she pointed out, 'they'll still be there outside the house. I think we should face them and get it over and done with.'

'Yes. I'll make a statement, tell them that's their lot and that will be that,' I agreed.

Driving into the quiet village we could see three cars parked outside our house. As we approached, the car doors flew open and a horde of reporters and photographers jumped out and ran over to us, cameras clicking and flashing round the car windows as we drew into our parking place beside the church. We climbed out and they all began shouting, asking us to look into their cameras and answer all their questions at once.

'Hallo.' I forced myself to smile. 'How nice to see you all. You must have been very uncomfortable sitting around here all this time.'

'Can you put your arm round Mrs Cook, Colonel?' someone shouted.

'We are just going to carry on as normal,' I said, 'but do take pictures if you like.'

'Can we have a statement?'

'What do you want to know? There's no story really. I'm back and life goes on.' In fact they were all fairly courteous and I felt quite sorry for them. I thought what an awful job they had, living off other people's misfortunes like vultures.

Inside the house there was an enormous bunch of flowers waiting for Caroline from Annie Leask to say sorry. I could not believe that a reporter could assassinate someone and then expect to be forgiven in such a way in the course of just a few hours. I wanted to throw them into the river but Caroline was touched by her apparent sincerity.

Once we had had time to reflect on the story in the *Express* and study the photographs, Marina and I had realized that they must have got their initial information from one of my soldiers who had helped us at the start, which was very disappointing. Marina remembered one of them taking that particular photograph of her at the party in her flat on the Saturday night before the Liberation Day, when the Crown Prince of Jordan visited. Only a soldier could have given them that picture. They also had the information about her illness because another of the soldiers had discovered her tablets at that party and had asked her what they were for: they had all heard about what was wrong with her, and these details appeared in the story. They would also have known that we spent a lot of time together since I am sure it was general barrack-room gossip. My driver, for instance, knew my movements exactly. Annie Leask did later admit to Caroline that it was one of the soldiers who sold the story to the *Express* in the first place, but she said that he was not paid very much money for it. The bomb, which had been ticking away for so long, had well and truly exploded. The paper spun the story out for a couple more days after the initial headline, reporting my return home, and then it seemed to wither away, with none of the other media bothering to follow it up.

Our son Edward was at Sandhurst at this time, on a training course. I had called Sandhurst from the caravan on the night that I heard what was happening, to warn him of what was coming so that he would not have to learn of it from the papers. He was actually out on an exercise when I rang but I managed to find one of his instructors and asked him to relay the message. William was in Australia, so we thought he was safely out of the way. We had no idea how to contact him anyway. Most of the time he was staying on his own in a tent beside rivers, or back-packing from one place to another. The last time we had heard from him, he had been staying with Maureen and Brian Douglas, the New Zealand couple who had been raising money for us, but we knew he had left them some while before. By this time he had been away for eight months. Caroline did not want to tell him. in any case, because she thought that if he knew he would be on the next plane home to comfort her, which would ruin his great trip. So the initial task of comforting and encouraging Caroline had been left to poor Edward. On the day after I returned, he was due to have a weekend break, so I drove to Sandhurst to pick him up.

Early one morning a few days later we received a call from Brian Douglas in New Zealand to say that he thought we should know that our name was in the papers down there. Apparently the *Express* goes out to a number of Commonwealth countries as the *World Express* once a week.

'I really advise,' Brian went on, 'that you get hold of William, because he is quite likely to see the story in Australia. I think he's on his way to stay with some relatives of ours whose names we gave him. Perhaps you should leave a message for him to ring you when he arrives.'

We took his advice and explained to the people what was happening. A few days later he rang. We had not heard from him for some weeks so it was nice to talk to him. He was not fishing in Australia because it was out of season, but he had been working on a farm, culling kangaroos and looking round the eastern coast and the Great Barrier Reef. Caroline had been alarmed recently by a story of a man being eaten by a crocodile out there, so she was doubly relieved to hear from him. We were both talking to him at the same time on different extensions.

'Have you seen the newspapers recently, Will?' I asked.

He laughed. 'I don't have much time for that sort of thing at the moment.'

'You ought to be aware that there is an unpleasant story in the press about me and Marina, the doctor in Croatia. I'm very, very sorry that it has happened and that it's got into the press. We didn't tell you before because we didn't want to spoil your trip, but it's all over now, I'm home with Mummy and everything's fine. It's happened and I'm sorry, please try to understand that I got very emotionally involved in the whole thing, but there is no need for you to worry about anything now.'

There was a long silence as he digested this news, and then he eventually spoke: 'I am not impressed.' I felt rather small and very foolish.

We chatted on rather tensely about what he had been doing and the conversation started to wind down. Then Caroline unwittingly diffused the tension as we said goodbye by saying, 'And darling, do beware of the crocodiles!' which made all three of us burst out laughing.

I was still officially in the army at this stage, although they were studiously ignoring me. I would have had to come back to England at some stage anyway for my final medicals and to attend a resettlement course, which everyone does when they leave the army. You have a choice of what courses you want to do and I opted for one called the 'bricks and mortar course'. I am the world's most impractical person, but this course is supposed to teach you how to effect minor repairs around the house so that you do not have to keep calling out builders, electricians and plumbers and spending money unnecessarily. It is a well-run course that has been going for many years. I spent three weeks on it at Aldershot and had a lot of fun with the other attendees. The irony of me doing a bricks and mortar course while building a million-pound orphanage was not lost on my friends.

The rest of my time was spent going flat out to try to raise the last bit of money that we needed. By then I had exhausted the possibilities of raising money from the people coming through Lipik, so England was the right place for me to be to get to the people with the money I needed. My last day in the army was 14 August; from then on I was officially a civilian, with no noticeable change in my daily life, except that now I was a pensioner, without a job, and so I immediately signed up and went on the dole. No one in the army spoke to me, either to congratulate me on my efforts in Lipik or to tell me off for my indiscretions. They simply ignored me and probably sighed with relief when I disappeared.

When I was last in England, during the spring, Caroline and I had been up in London and had bumped into an old friend called Sally Basely coming out of Fortnum and Mason's. She had worked at the Hilton in Hong Kong when we were there twenty-five years before and we had not seen her since. We all recognized each other immediately, however, and she had heard about the project. We chatted about it for a while.

'I work for a very wealthy Greek shipping tycoon,' she said, 'with this enormous house in St James's. He loves children and he's also a friend of Prince Alexander of Yugoslavia, who lives in London. I'm sure the Prince would like to meet you, would you like an introduction?'

'Yes, please.' I accepted unhesitatingly. If there was one thing I had learnt about fund-raising it was that you can never have too many influential contacts and you have to follow every lead until it comes to a dead end.

Sally rang a few days later and said the Prince would like me to call him and she gave me his telephone number. He was very charming and invited Sally and me to lunch at a Chinese restaurant in London. After lunch we went back to his office and met his wife, who was also working as a fund-raiser for various causes in former Yugoslavia. She gave me two names and addresses of people she thought might be useful to me. One was a man who was the International Director of the Variety Club of Great Britain and the other was a lady in Italy who was the wife of one of their ex-prime ministers and was also involved in fund-raising. I wrote to both of them.

Two days later I got a wildly enthusiastic call from the Variety Club man. He was just about to go to America for a conference and wanted all the details to take with him. These I sent off to him immediately as he was convinced they would be willing to give us some money. I tried contacting him many times after he was due back but never heard another word from him. By now I had grown accustomed to these sorts of dead-ends and disappointments, and realized that they were part and parcel of the fund-raising business. For every hundred leads that come to nothing, perhaps one will produce something, or lead on to something even better.

I subsequently received a call from an American who was working for the Italian ex-prime minister's wife as her fund-raiser. He too wanted more details, which I faxed through. Not only did he have the decency to come back to me to explain that it was not something they could help with, but he went on to say, 'Look, I have a lot of experience of fund-raising. Let's talk and maybe I can give you a fresh idea or two.' Eventually he said, 'What you want to do is contact the top advertising agencies in London, tell them your story and see if they will donate you some free advertising space. We do this all the time in America.'

It sounded like a good idea, except that I did not know anybody in the advertising world. Then I remembered a man called Nigel Clark who was married to an old girlfriend of mine whom I had not seen for twenty-five years, but whose daughter had shared a flat with our son Edward in Bristol, another amazing coincidence. I rang him and told him my story.

'Can you help?' I asked.

'No, sorry,' he replied. 'They do that sort of thing in America, but it doesn't work over here. No one gives free space away. But I have an idea. Give me five minutes and I'll ring you back.' Five minutes later he did so. 'Have you ever heard of a programme called *Hearts of Gold*?'

'No.'

'It's an Esther Rantzen programme, a bit like *This is Your Life*, but concentrating on people who do good work, telling their stories. I have a very good friend who knows Esther Rantzen. I've told him the story and he's going to tell her about it. Send me all the details you have.'

So I got back to the fax machine, and afterwards forgot all about it. There were plenty of things to distract my attention.

A few weeks later the phone rang. It was a man called Julian Beynon from the BBC. 'We are launching a new programme,' he explained, 'on small charities and the problems of fund-raising. May I come down and see you?'

'Oh, don't worry about that,' I said. 'I'm often up in London, I'll come and see you.'

'No, no,' he insisted, 'I love getting out of the office. I'll come down to you.'

'It seems a long way to come just to chat.'

'We just want to see if yours is the sort of story that we might be interested in. I'm a freelance, you see, so I have to convince my boss that it is a story worth telling.'

I agreed, and later in the week he turned up and talked for about two hours. He seemed to want to know every detail. A few days later he called back to say they were very keen. 'Can we come down and do a filmed interview next week?'

A big crew duly arrived at the house and set things up in the drawing room, with a big coloured screen behind me. They explained this was to cut out some of the clutter of the bookshelves and pictures behind. They then told me that I had the wrong-coloured shirt on and after about three changes I found a green one they were happy with. We did the interview, in which I became quite emotional while talking about Lipik and the children, and they seemed very pleased with it. They took a few photographs of me in the study writing letters and left, saying that they thought it would be broadcast sometime in the autumn.

'The earlier you can do it, the better,' I said, 'because we really need some money fast. We have a lot of bills to pay out there and by the autumn the whole project should be finished.'

Julian rang the following week to tell me that it was going to be shown on a Sunday night at peak viewing time in

October, which was later than I hoped, but it was to be the first in the new series.

All this time I was keeping in touch with Ivan and Goran by phone and fax, following how things were going on site. I felt very sad not to be part of it, and very left out. It was as if my life was taking place without me. But I knew I had to stay away. I did not contact Marina. I wrote hundreds of letters to people I hoped would donate, and with each letter I felt I was somehow keeping in touch with Lipik and, indirectly, with Marina. I felt miserable.

William returned from his fishing trip on 30 August and Caroline, Edward and I went up as a family with Jess, our dog, to meet him at Heathrow. He looked wonderful. He had left ten months before with very short hair and had returned with flowing locks and a deep tan. It's a cliché, I know, but he had gone away a boy and returned a man, having had many amazing experiences: working as a guide on the rivers in Chile, camping on his own by rivers in New Zealand and farming in Australia and South Africa, looking after himself, living on his wits out of a pack.

A few days after he got back, he and I walked by the River Wylye beside our house in the evening with our fishing rods. I knew he wanted to talk about what had happened and I had been reluctant to start the conversation. 'So what exactly happened in Croatia?' he eventually asked. 'I'd like to know.'

It was easy to forget that he had missed the whole thing. Whereas Edward had seen the complications develop, hearing each piece of news at virtually the same time as Caroline, and had seen Lipik and met Marina and the children, William had none of this background.

It was somehow easier to talk with the distraction of the fishing to cover the more difficult moments. I explained about how I had become emotionally entangled with the destruction and the suffering in Croatia and Lipik, how I had become involved with the children and how Marina had been part of all those things. 'I am desperately sorry for all the hurt I have caused Mummy. It has been a horribly painful time for many people, but particularly for her. But it's all over now and behind us. I promise.' At that moment I truly believed that it *was* all over, and I felt absolutely wretched.

Caroline could see how unhappy I was at being stuck in England while the project went ahead without me, and eventually we agreed that I should go back there for a few days, just to see what was going on and to make sure that things were happening as they should be. I cannot imagine how hard it must have been for her to agree to that, but for me it felt like a lead weight being lifted off my chest. I could breathe freely again. 'Promise me you'll come back,' she said.

'I promise.'

I flew down on Saturday, 11 September and booked a return flight for Thursday the 16th. On the night of the 16th I was due to talk to Sherborne Girls' School and Caroline was confident that I would not want to let them down.

On the Friday before leaving I rang Goran. 'How is it going?' I asked.

'Oh, it is great, Mark. I wish you could come out and see it.'

'Well, I am, I'm flying out tomorrow.'

'What? What?'

'Will you pick me up from the airport?'

'Yes, of course. That is fantastic!'

'Can you book me a bed in the hospital?'

'No, you must stay with us at home.'

It was kind of him, but I knew he had enough problems, still not having running water in the flat and with two small children to worry about. 'No,' I insisted, 'I will stay at the hospital.' I knew he was only being polite and was relieved that I did not take him up on the offer. We chatted on for a few minutes.

'This is such good news,' he said. 'What a pity Marina is going away on her summer holidays.'

'When is she going?' I tried to keep my voice light.

'Tomorrow morning, I think.'

'Where is she going?'

'I don't know, she won't tell anyone where she is going, just holidays.'

I felt the lead weight land back on my chest.

16

Ambushed by Esther

Goran showed me proudly round the site and I was amazed by how much had happened since I had been away. The crane had gone now, the roof was on, and they were beginning to paint the walls a soft pink colour. There was still a lot of building machinery around but we now had three beautiful buildings standing among the trees. Between them were immaculately laid paths and terraces of pink and yellow bricks. Where there had been a cratered playing field there was now a level, resurfaced pitch. There were new seats dotted around, overlooking the grounds.

My visit was also timed to coincide with an enormous aid convoy arriving from England. It was reputed to be the largest convoy of aid ever to leave Britain, consisting of over fifty vehicles. It had been organized by the Walsall Police Force, and Lipik was to be just one of the stops on their tour. The organizer, Chief Inspector Leslie Leek, had contacted me a few weeks before to tell me they were going out and to ask if there was anything we needed.

'That's very kind,' I said. 'Can you give me a little time to think about it?'

Some months earlier Marino the Mayor and Marina had told me that they needed a fire engine, a hearse and a dust cart for the town, their old ones having been destroyed in the war. I had mentioned it to one or two people who had made inquiries about aid, but nothing had happened so far. For most people it was rather a tall order. When Leslie rang me in England I thought that he might know people in the emergency aid services who could provide this sort of equipment. I sent him a fax, thanking him for the offer and telling him we needed these three things, ending, 'This is not a joke.'

Half an hour later he came on the phone. 'Got your fax,' he said. 'That's a bit of challenge, isn't it? I like a challenge. I'll see what I can do.' A few days later he came back to tell me he had the fire engine and the hearse, but was having trouble finding a dust cart. Two out of three was an extremely impressive result for such a difficult task and I thought it was important that I should be in Lipik to receive them officially when they arrived. The convoy was a major effort on their behalf and deserved recognition.

They reached Zagreb on the Sunday night and headed for Lipik on the Tuesday. I met them at the UN checkpoint and climbed into the fire engine, which was the lead vehicle, to guide them into town. I had arranged with Marino the Mayor that I would bring the vehicles to the front of the ruins of the elegant Kursalon, the symbol of Lipik. There would be a reception committee of children, old people and refugees from the hospital on the steps of the Kursalon to greet them before we went into the hospital for a big lunch and the official handover to Marino with speeches and handshakings. We drove into town with all sirens blaring.

The amount of effort involved in mounting an operation like this is enormous. For instance, there was one policewoman in the convoy, from the Falkland Islands, who had raised £2,000 herself, 'indulged' on an RAF flight to the UK, bought £2,000-worth of stores, loaded them on to a lorry and then joined the convoy so that she could hand the goods over personally. That was a very impressive personal achievement.

As the convoy moved on after lunch, and peace descended once more on the town, Goran came over to me. 'I have a telephone message for you,' he said casually, as if it had almost slipped his mind, which telephone messages frequently did, 'from Marina. She is coming back from holiday early and she would like to meet you in Zagreb tomorrow evening.' My heart leaped. It had now been three months since I had spoken to her, since we parted in her surgery and I bumped away in Ivan's car. I was desperate to see her.

I was due to fly home on the Thursday morning and Goran and I were planning to spend the next day in Zagreb anyway, meeting with Government officials and The Knights of Malta, a humanitarian aid organization. In the evening I was due to go to the Intercontinental Hotel to meet David Grubb, the boss of Feed the Children. I was thinking about trying to join the organization myself now that my role in Lipik was winding down. I had had a lot of dealings with them and they impressed me as a very well-run, small aid organization and I wanted to find out if they would be able to use my services in any way.

I arranged to meet Marina once all this activity was over, at nine o'clock in the evening, under 'the tail of the horse', a statue which we both knew in the main square of the city. It was hard to keep my mind on what people were saying to me throughout the day as I watched the minutes tick slowly by. When I finally got to the statue she was already waiting, but she was accompanied by a man and a woman, friends of hers from Mostar. I could not believe that there was going to be yet another delay before we could be alone together. The deadline for my departure in the morning was looming ever closer and I resented wasting another minute of the time on anyone else. The man was the boss of a big furniture company and he was extremely keen to get the contract for furnishing the orphanage. I felt like screaming, but I continued to act as if nothing was wrong, all the time seething with impatience. It was a warm evening, so we sat at one of the many tables set outside the restaurants and coffee bars surrounding the square, drinking and talking. Eventually the other couple went, leaving Marina and me together at last. She was looking her very best, with no evidence of any trouble with her skin. She told me she had seen a specialist, who had prescribed some new drugs which had got her illness under better control.

We spent the rest of the night talking, not wanting to waste any of the precious hours on sleep, firstly at the café table and then in her car. Over the months I had grown fond of that tinny little white Yugo. Hardly anything about it worked properly but it kept going somehow. Every time we drove it at night a policeman would flag us down somewhere or other to tell us that one of the headlights was not working, but we never seemed to get round to fixing it. Marina had had the car since she was a student in Sarajevo and was fiercely proud of it, as she was of her dreadful driving.

We talked about everything we had done since our last meeting, about how we felt and what was happening in our lives. As the sun came up we drove to her aunt's flat to collect Snoopy, who seemed as ecstatic to see me as I was to see him, and took him for a walk in the park. We then drove to the airport, having another coffee while we waited for my plane.

As I left her yet again to board my flight I felt as though I was being torn in half, but I was in no position to make any promises or commitments for the future. I was living from day to day, with no idea what would happen next. 'I hope I will see you again very soon,' I said formally as we said goodbye. I was so confused about everything. She obviously still loved me, despite the fact that I had been away for so long without a word of contact, and I knew that I still loved her. What I did not know was what I was going to do about it.

Exhausted from lack of sleep, I had to prepare my presentation for Sherborne Girls' School on the plane. I had been talking to a lot of schools in the last few months to raise money, and I wanted this one to be particularly good since it had been arranged by Anne Dixon, our neighbour and friend, and we also knew several girls at the school, which meant that word on my performance would spread quickly. When I got home there was only time to prepare slides and videos before we set off for the school, taking Edward, William and a friend of theirs, who had also been to Sherborne, with us.

We prepared the hall very carefully and I rehearsed the boys so that we could give a very slick presentation with videos, slides and maps all appearing and disappearing with military precision as I snapped my fingers. I was always keen to use maps in these presentations, to bring home to the children just how close to them this was happening. I remembered how shocked I had been to find that Zagreb was only two hours' flying time from London and I wanted to get this across to my audiences. This was not happening in Outer Mongolia, but in the heart of Europe. Many of the Sherborne girls had been on holiday to countries like Italy and Austria, which were right next door to Croatia. In this case I was able to illustrate the point by telling them that just that morning I had been in Zagreb and now I was here with them.

We had dinner with the headmistress and some other guests before going on stage. By then I was getting a second wind, perhaps because I was talking about the subject which I loved more than anything. It all went extremely smoothly and I was very proud of the boys. There were about 500 pupils in the audience and we obviously impressed them because they collected a lot of money and afterwards we were surrounded by eager, excited girls, all wanting to do more, including going out to Lipik in their holidays, and some of them donated Snoopy duvet covers and pillow cases for the children.

So the evening went well, despite the fact that I was dazed with tiredness and completely disoriented emotionally. It had been wonderful to see and talk with Marina again, and the night had flown by. In some ways it seemed as if I had not been away but now I felt more confused than ever. I found that I could not go back to being completely out of contact with her and began to make surreptitious phone calls to her whenever I got the chance. I took stupid risks, tempting fate all the time.

Soon Edward was going back to the University of the West of England in Bristol, having decided that Sandhurst and the army were not for him after all. William was now due to start at St Andrews University in Scotland, so Caroline and I arranged to drive him up there.

The day before we left there was a memorial service for a young man called Dan Eldon at St Bride's Church in Fleet Street. I had been contacted a few weeks before by his mother, Kathy Eldon. She rang me from Los Angeles to say that her son Dan, a photographer, had been killed in Somalia, and I remembered reading the sad story. American troops had gone after the rebel leader General Aidid in a big helicopter operation in Mogadishu and had accidentally killed many Somali civilians. The people had been so angry that they had turned on any white people they could find and had killed four reporters. One of them was twenty-two-year-old Dan Eldon, who had been working as a photographer for Reuters. He was obviously a very remarkable young man who had done a great deal to help others, particularly children, in his short life. His mother wanted to start up a charity in his memory and she also wanted to donate his Land-Rover to a good cause and wondered if I would be interested. I said that we would very much like to have it and she asked if we would mind co-operating on some publicity which should benefit us and the Dan Eldon Memorial Trust at the same time.

I was delighted to agree and went to London to meet a group of young journalists and publicists who were organizing everything. They seemed an enthusiastic and good-hearted bunch, and I had no way of knowing how much damage they would cause in my life in a few months' time. The Land-Rover was about twenty years old and needed quite a bit of work, but they had found a garage that would provide the labour free, and Unipart were giving the parts. We decided to call it 'Dan's Van' and the organizers planned to drive it overland to Lipik themselves.

The service in St Bride's was for all four reporters. It was extremely beautiful and very moving with wonderful music, addresses and readings. Dan's younger sister, Amy, spoke with great pride about her brother and the good he had done in his life. I felt very sad that I had never met him.

Before I went back to Lipik I had been telephoned by a woman who ran a public relations company called Kerr-Smiley PR Ltd. She wanted me to open a new art gallery in London on Monday, 3 October, which was when I was due to be in Scotland with Caroline and William.

'Why me?' I asked.

'The first exhibition is going to be photographs of children,' Nony Kerr-Smiley explained. 'One of the exhibitors is the *Daily Mail* photographer, Steve Back, who took pictures of you and the children in Croatia last year. He has suggested you would be suitable to open it because of the work you are doing with children.'

'I'm sorry, but I'm afraid I am going to be in Scotland that weekend, taking my son up to university, and then my wife and I are having some time off up there. I'm afraid I have promised.'

'Oh dear.' She sounded very crestfallen. 'Is there any way you think you could do it? I mean, we will fly you down for it if that's necessary, and then get you back in time for your holiday.'

'That's a bit expensive just for opening an art gallery, isn't it?'

'Honestly, we do want you to do it,' she insisted. 'There will be a lot of press there, including *Newsround* from the BBC, so you would get a lot of publicity for the orphanage. I know you need more money and this would be a wonderful opportunity.'

'I'm sorry.' She was making it sound tempting but I felt I had to hold out. I knew that Caroline would not be thrilled if I disappeared on the first day of our holiday to publicize Lipik. 'I'll give it some thought, though.' *Newsround*, the children's news programme, would be an ideal opportunity to talk about the project, and children are always the best fund-raisers if they take a cause to their hearts.

'Please do.'

I did not mention the conversation to Caroline, feeling sure

I knew how she would react. We were supposed to be making a clean break, getting away from telephones and faxes, not thinking about Croatia or Lipik or any of it. I could not ask her to agree to this. Caroline knew I was on edge after my return from the latest trip and we were both being very careful with each other. That evening, while we were getting supper, Caroline casually asked what the phone call had been about, having overheard parts of it. 'Don't worry,' I said, 'just some PR woman who wants me to open an art gallery.'

'Tell me about it.' So I told her and she looked thoughtful. 'Do you think it would help you raise money?'

'It probably would,' I said reluctantly. 'They say *Newsround* is going to be there and children are always good money-raisers.'

'If they are willing to fly you up and down, why don't you do it? I don't mind as long as we all drive up together. We could drive up on the Friday and stay with the Watts on the way up, then on to Edinburgh, have lunch with the Steels. You could fly back, leaving me with them for the night, and you come back on Monday.'

'Are you sure you don't mind?'

'I don't mind, as long as you promise to come straight back up afterwards.'

'We do need the money.' Her attitude was coming as something of a relief to me. 'It would be a good opportunity.'

'I really think you should do it,' she said in a voice which suggested she wanted to hear no more argument on the subject.

So the next day I rang Nony Kerr-Smiley and told her I would do it. She was more than delighted and proved to be remarkably efficient about sending me all the tickets and itineraries I needed. On the way up to Scotland we stopped in Lancashire to stay with our great friends the Watts, whom we had known for nearly thirty years. He and I had been in the Gurkhas together and now we were both retired. The following morning we drove on to other Gurkha friends, the Steels, in Edinburgh. Halfway there Caroline realized she had left her handbag behind, 'with everything in it'. I was not bothered as we were going to be stopping off there again on the way back and I had all the money we needed for the holiday. She seemed unduly anxious, however, and dashed off to phone the Watts the moment we arrived in Edinburgh, to check the bag was there. She seemed to calm down after that. We all had lunch and I rushed to the airport to catch the shuttle back south. On the way I took a wrong turning and nearly missed the plane, but I made it just in time and flew down to London.

A chauffeur met me at the airport and took me to the Wembley Hilton Hotel. Nony Kerr-Smiley was due to pick me up at eight o'clock 'on the dot'. Going up to my room to change, I took the opportunity to ring Marina in Lipik, to tell her what I was up to and find out her news. At about seven-thirty I went downstairs for a drink to brace myself for the event and to mull over what I would say in my short speech. Eight o'clock came and Nony did not arrive. I began to wonder what was happening. With about three minutes to spare before we were meant to be at the gallery, a car screamed up and she bundled me into it, blurting out apologies and excuses.

There was no time to think but she talked as we went. 'Actually there won't be many people there as it's the official opening, but the media will be there and the local mayor and mayoress, and some of the photographers who I will introduce you to, and a few other people.'

'How do I address the mayor and his wife in the speech?'

'I think it's Your Worship the Mayor and Lady Mayoress,' she said as the car screeched to a halt and she bundled me back out on to the pavement. There was a big white sign outside saying 'The New London Art Gallery'. We went in and someone pinned a microphone on my lapel for the *Newsround* sound team. I was hustled along a corridor into the gallery and introduced to the mayor, who was wearing all his chains and finery. I noticed the hairs on his chest poking through, because he had no tie on, which struck me as odd, but I assumed that mayors were more casual these days in London – I was becoming more accepting of these sorts of eccentricities now, I told myself. I was introduced to several more people and then Nony Kerr-Smiley asked if I would mind getting straight on to the podium and saying my few words. I was rather taken aback and confused at the rush of the whole thing, but did as I was asked and started my speech.

'Your Worship the Mayor, Lady Mayoress . . .'

'Oh, Colonel Cook,' she interrupted me again, 'I'm so sorry, I nearly forgot, we've got a special message for you from someone who regrets very much that they can't be here tonight.' At that point I noticed a television set beside her which was flickering into life, and for a confusing moment I thought I was about to be confronted with Marina, but instead of that Martin Bell's face came up on the screen.

'Hallo, Mark,' he said, 'I'm sorry I can't be with you tonight. You are not in fact here to open an art gallery as you think, you are here to appear on the *Hearts of Gold* programme.'

The screen then filled with pictures of Lipik and the orphanage, followed by the interview which Julian Beynon had done weeks before at our home, with images of the town and the children filling the screen that he had insisted on putting behind me. On top of that was some highly emotional church music which I later discovered was Fauré's lovely *Cantique de Jean Racine*. I was dazed, horribly embarrassed, confused and shocked. They kept showing pictures of my reactions in a little heart on the corner of the screen. After a few minutes the film stopped, a disembodied voice announced, 'Colonel Cook, you are on *Hearts of Gold*', and the whole wall of the gallery slid back to reveal a full-sized television studio, complete with an audience applauding like mad and Esther

Rantzen approaching me with a broad grin. To add to the shock, there on the stage were Caroline, Edward and William. Caroline and William, I discovered later, had been on the next plane after me from Edinburgh. Had I missed my flight I would have bumped into them. The details of the flight and vital contact telephone numbers had been in the handbag which Caroline had been so worried about leaving behind in Lancashire, but at that moment none of it made any sense at all to me.

She and the boys had known about the programme for many weeks and had been part of the subterfuge. This explained why she was happy for me to alter the holiday plans, just to 'open an art gallery'. Under the circumstances it was amazing that she managed to keep the secret from me and had been so co-operative with the BBC. She could so easily have destroyed the event at a very early stage, in which case it would have been cancelled and I would have lost my 'moment of glory' and the thousands of pounds that it raised.

I also discovered later that Esther Rantzen knew that Caroline and I were going through a difficult time and she hoped that by including her and the boys in the programme it would help unite us. I was amazed and grateful for her thoughtfulness and concern.

At that moment, however, I was completely dazed. Esther interviewed me for a few seconds and then said, 'I understand you need some more money to finish the job.'

'Yes, a hell of a lot, actually,' I agreed.

'How much?'

'About a quarter of a million pounds.'

'Well,' she said, 'we wondered how we could help you, and we've come up with an idea.' At that point a large television screen showed the production of a calendar in fast motion. Then her colleague, Mike Smith, drove a forklift truck into the studio, carrying a crate of the calendars. They had done the most extraordinary thing. They had approached top photographers, including Lords Snowdon and Lichfield, Steve

Back, Koo Stark and others, and asked them to donate their favourite pictures of children. They had then had 20,000 calendars made up with the pictures. Everything involved, including the printing and the paper, had been donated free, and Woolworths had agreed to sell the calendars, with every penny coming to the orphanage. It was a wonderful idea and I was dumbstruck. The calendars were beautifully produced, with Steve Back's picture of Vladek and Valentina on the front. 'Do you know the children in this picture?' Esther asked.

'Yes, I know them well.'

'Who are they?'

'That's Valentina,' I said, 'and that's Daniel.'

'Are you sure it's Daniel?' For a moment she seemed to falter and I realized what I had said.

'No, of course not. I'm so sorry. That's his twin brother, Vladek.'

'So where do you think Vladek is now?'

'Well, I hope he's tucked up in his bed in Croatia.'

'No, he's not,' she crowed happily. 'Look behind you.' And sure enough, as I turned I saw Vladek and Goran coming towards me. Vladek ran across to me and I lifted him up into my arms.

'I think, Vladek,' Esther said when I had put him down again, embraced Goran and recovered a little from the shock, 'you have something you would like to say to Colonel Cook.'

Vladek looked up at me with his huge eyes and, in perfectly rehearsed English, said, 'Thank you, Mark,' and pinned a Heart of Gold on my chest. The music swelled, the crowd applauded. I felt the tears welling up and the heart fell to the ground. The director's disembodied voice came over the speakers. 'Can we do it again, to get the boy's name right.'

Fame

Everyone in the audience wanted to buy calendars, and they all wanted Vladek and me to autograph them. The two of us sat down at a table and spent the next hour or so just signing and smiling. Vladek attacked the task with the utmost serious-ness and dignity, giving every signature his most careful attention, the perfect instant star.

One of the contributing photographers who was not able to get there was Steve Back, as he was halfway up Mount Everest at the time, which was a great shame since it had been his pictures which had started the whole thing off. He was represented by a reporter from the *Daily Mail* who conveyed his regrets and asked if we could have a chat to update the story since the last time it appeared in the *Mail*.

'I only need about half an hour,' she assured me.

'Well, I can't do it just now.' I gestured towards the queue for autographs.

'Could I come back to the hotel with you afterwards and do it?'

'Yes, okay.' I reluctantly agreed since she was so insistent.

Later, when we had finished at the studio, Caroline and I, Edward, William, Goran and Vladek all headed back to the Wembley Hilton with some of the other people involved in the programme and the reporter followed us into reception. 'Could we do the interview now?' she inquired.

'Yes.' I was being cautious. 'As long as we are only talking about the orphanage.'

'Yes, of course, that's all we're interested in.'

So we sat down to chat over the beers and sandwiches which were being served, while everyone else milled around us. The questions started innocuously enough. It was an awkward time to be trying to concentrate on one person when there were so many other people I wanted to talk to. She seemed to be going on for ever, and then, after about an hour, she started slipping in personal questions. 'Tell me,' she wheedled, 'is everything all right with your wife now? You're happy?'

I began to grow impatient and the atmosphere turned ugly. Caroline and the boys were also becoming angry and the wonderful high spirits which the show had created evaporated into exasperation and unpleasantness. It appeared that I just had not learnt my lesson. Tabloid news reporters seem only to want nasty stories and our evening was ruined as a result. Then Caroline went to the reception desk for our room key and discovered that I had made a call from the room earlier. Her suspicions immediately aroused, she asked for a print-out of the details, which showed her exactly what number I had called and for how long I had talked. By the time we got to the privacy of our room she was boiling with anger and fighting hard to try to control herself. I had to leave the room to talk to the BBC people for a few minutes later on, and when I returned I discovered that the Heart of Gold had been hurled across the room, followed by my own copy of the calendar. I could hardly be surprised by this reaction, especially as she had particularly asked me before I left Edinburgh not to ring Marina.

We were due to fly back to Scotland at lunch-time the next day, so we had a morning to fill. It was cold but pleasant and we all decided to take Vladek to London Zoo. The *Daily Mail* sent a photographer to get pictures of him with the animals to accompany the story, which they still promised was going to be positive coverage for the orphanage. I was willing to agree to that because I thought that innocent pictures of an orphan playing with animals would offset anything unpleasant they might put in the text, but having to stop and pose every few yards spoiled the morning. In the end the article was never printed anyway.

The *Hearts of Gold* team were all most impressive from start to finish, leaving aside the intrinsic deviousness of their operation. Julian Beynon in particular seemed to have constructed the whole event with the most immaculate use of subterfuge and split-second timing. It was a masterpiece of military planning, getting so many people to the right places at the right times, organizing a passport for Vladek, and then getting him and Goran past some very suspicious Immigration officials. They were fantastically well organized and very nice people. We all had a snack lunch at the hotel before Edward headed back to Bristol and Caroline, William and I to Scotland. Goran and Vladek were staying on for another day as the guests of the BBC. That afternoon they were taken to Wembley Stadium, which fascinated Goran, who is a graduate in physical training, and Vladek was photographed holding the FA Cup.

By the time the *Hearts of Gold* programme was broadcast on Tuesday night, Caroline and I were in St Andrews to drop off William. We were watching in the hotel with the Brewsters, a couple we had known since our days in Brunei, which was appropriate as Caro Brewster was one of the project's most tireless fund-raisers. At the end of the programme they announced that the calendars would be on sale at Woolworths throughout the United Kingdom from the next day.

Wednesday was a wet, grey, windy day in St Andrews, but Caroline and I decided to go down to the local Woolworths to see if the calendars were there. We reckoned that if they had managed to get to that distant branch they should be everywhere. Sure enough, we found a whole pile of them. We loitered around the counter for a while, pretending to look at things on the surrounding shelves, and watched as people picked them up and walked to the till as casually as if they were buying their morning newspapers. One woman helped herself to three, turned to me and said casually, 'Would you mind signing these for me?'

After dropping William at the university, Caroline and I finally set off for our two-week holiday in Scotland. We decided to use B roads and go exploring as we made our way around the various friends we wanted to visit. We were going to see all the people in Scotland who had helped with the project, to thank them personally and let them know what was happening to all their money. It was still rather grey and drizzly, and after an hour or two of driving we decided to stop the car and consult the map. It was a very quiet road and only one car went past us in the opposite direction. We were deep in discussion when a knock on the steamed-up window made me jump. I wound it down to find a woman outside with a £5 note in her hand.

'I saw you on television last night,' she said, handing the note through the window, 'I'd like to give you this for your orphanage.'

'How on earth did you recognize us through all the rain?'

'It was my daughter, actually. She recognized you as we drove past.'

'That's remarkable.'

'She's adopted, you see, so the story had a great effect on her.'

'Where is she?'

'She's in the car. She's too shy to come out.' So I went to thank the girl, who was curled up with embarrassment.

One of the people we visited on this holiday was my old school chaplain, the Reverend Tony Pepper, whom I had not seen for thirty-five years. He had been following the project ever since Martin Bell was shot and I had announced to the world that I had been to school with him and was building an orphanage. Apparently the event was reported in the school magazine and Tony had raised money and aid in his parish to send to us throughout the following months. It was marvellous people like this who helped us to keep going at times when we could have become dispirited and thought we could not go on. The wonderful letters of encouragement that they sent with their donations had so often lifted our spirits and made us realize that we were not struggling on our own.

On the way back we stopped at the Thorneyholme Hall Health Spa as the manager, Paula Dumas-Rimmel, had managed to collect £2,000 for us. Caroline and I spent a very pleasant afternoon being massaged and snoozing in sauna baths before receiving the cheque.

When we arrived home there was a phone call from a young couple running a hospitality company called Fortesqueue's. They had seen *Hearts of Gold* and they wanted to organize a charity ball for us in London. I was rather lukewarm about the idea, feeling that I had enough on my plate without worrying about a formal ball.

'Please can we just come down to talk to you about it?' they persisted, and I agreed.

They came to lunch and they were so enthusiastic, dynamic and full of ideas that they swept Caroline and me along with them. They promised that they would take care of everything and all we would have to do was turn up on the night and accept the money. It seemed churlish not to agree to let them do it. The idea was to have the ball on Saturday, 11 December. Because it was rather short notice to arrange such a large event they had to work fantastically hard, and printed up beautiful invitations with pictures of the children on. They needed to sell a minimum of twenty tables with ten people per table, and there would be an auction in the middle for prizes like Wimbledon tickets, which had already been donated. It was a good idea, but within a few weeks it began to look as if we would not get sufficient numbers of people. Panic set in and the organizers started searching around for public relations opportunities to promote the event and stimulate ticket sales. I felt very sorry for them, because they were working so hard, and I promised to do whatever interviews they could organize.

I now found myself unable to resist telephoning Marina whenever I had a chance, promising Caroline that I was doing no such thing. What I did not realize was that a new telephone exchange had been installed in our area and that we were due to receive itemized phone bills. The first incriminating list of numbers fell out of its envelope on to the breakfast table. I palmed the offending pages like a cheating schoolboy and slid them under the cushion on my chair while Caroline was distracted by the telephone ringing. I had not had time to notice that the pages were numbered, and Caroline had spotted my guilty action anyway. She demanded that I produce the missing pages and after a few hopeless denials I was forced to comply. Every call I had made, sometimes several in one day to the same number, was recorded.

Caroline exploded. 'Just get out!' she yelled at me. We circled each other in the kitchen for a while, trying to talk. She realized that if I did go it would all be over and there would be no going back, so we soldiered on. But now her suspicions were fully aroused she started to find faxes and notes which I had made pathetic attempts to hide everywhere.

The *Hearts of Gold* programme also brought another phone call from the *Daily Express* 'Hallo,' the voice said, 'my name is Phillipa Kennedy. I'm a features writer on the *Daily Express* and I would really like to do a piece on your work in Lipik.'

'You must be joking!' I burst out. 'Have you any idea what your paper has done to us?'

'No, please,' she interrupted before I could hang up, 'I'm a feature writer, nothing to do with the news pages. I would like to do something to make amends.' It turned out that she was actually the wife of an old army friend of mine and she did a delightful article about the *Hearts of Gold* calendars, with no mention of our private problems.

The 20,000 calendars sold out from Woolworths almost within twenty-four hours and there was clearly a demand for more. Esther Rantzen and her team very kindly arranged for a reprint, which must have meant a lot of work for them.

Apparently Esther Rantzen knows Mohammed Al-Fayed, who owns Harrods, and she sent him a tape of the show. He agreed to put up the money for the reprinting, because we could not really expect people like the printers and paper company to make yet another donation after being so generous the first time. He then put a further 20,000 calendars on sale in Harrods and other House of Fraser stores. When we were next in London Caroline and I went along to Harrods to meet and thank him. We were met by his very suave public relations man, Michael Cole, who said, 'Actually I know all about you because my wife knew you when you were a small boy in Lowestoft. I know all the good works you did as a child as well, so it didn't really surprise us that you have done this . . .'

As soon as we were on our own Caroline asked in an amused tone, 'What good works did you do as a child?'

'I've no idea,' I had to admit. 'I can't remember doing anything.'

By the end of November the building work was drawing to a close in Lipik and I realized that no one had actually made any decisions about the furnishings. The idea of concurrent activity seemed to be lost on Goran and his team, who were only now turning their minds to furniture. It had been my intention originally to equip the home with furniture donated to us, and the Red Cross had already offered me some old army beds. But by now the orphanage had become a symbol, not only of hope for the local people but also of international co-operation, and an indication of the will of the Croatian Government in Zagreb actually to do something really positive in this war-stricken area. Everyone involved wanted to do the job as well as possible.

'We must get an architect to come and measure up,' I was told over the phone.

'But we want the children back by Christmas.' I was appalled by this news. I could quite see another six months dragging by before the building was habitable. I felt that I needed to be there to keep things going or we were going to miss our deadline yet again.

'I really think I need to go back for one last push,' I told Caroline. 'I should only need a week to sort it out and get them moving.'

I could see that she was very nervous about this, and understandably so, but I felt it had to be done and she eventually, reluctantly, agreed. Two days before I was due to go, however, she received a telephone call from Ros Hardie, one of our Scottish fund-raising friends, who had just got back from taking aid to Lipik and had a lot of news. She had rung to tell us how well everything was going down there and how it was all nearly finished and looked fantastic. Caroline answered the phone and Ros was obviously telling her something else which seemed to surprise Caroline. I was half-listening to the conversation as I was doing something else. 'No,' Caroline was saying, 'I didn't know that. Yes, I suppose that is very good news.'

After a few minutes she handed the phone to me and Ros gave me an update on how the building was looking and how it had been inspected by the authorities and passed. We finished the conversation and I was still puzzled by what she had told Caroline which was such 'good news'. 'What did Ros tell you that surprised you?' I asked.

'I wonder what you will say if I tell you that Marina has a boyfriend and it seems to be quite serious.'

It was as if I had been punched in the stomach. My heart missed several beats. Although I had told Goran I was going out I had not told Marina. I was leaving the following day and suddenly I was dreading it.

18

A Rival

I rang Goran the night before I left, to check that he would be able to meet me at the airport. 'Sure, sure, no problem,' he assured me. 'It is a shame, you will be missing Marina again.'

I felt my fear deepen. 'Why?'

'She is away at a medical conference, somewhere on the coast.'

It seemed that things just got worse and worse.

When I arrived at Zagreb Goran was there, as always, and I tried not to talk too much about Marina and my disappointment. I felt that he had been involved enough in my personal affairs, it was very hard for him to be stuck in the middle, and I appreciated that. We had meetings in the city with the Government people about the money before driving back to Lipik that evening. I had supper with Goran and his family before retiring to my bed at the hospital.

I was roused from a deep sleep by a loud banging on the bedroom door. 'Open up, police! Open up!' I hauled myself back to consciousness and groped my way across to the door. I opened it, still only half-awake, and Marina was standing there, grinning mischievously. I was still hazy with sleep and could not work out what was happening. Slowly my memory came back to me.

'I thought you were at a conference.'

'I was. It finished today so I came home.'

'How did you know I was here?'

'I stopped in Selce to have supper with the children. Snježana told me you were here.'

'How did she know?'

'You saw Josipa, didn't you?'

I had seen Josipa that evening, a girl who had left the orphanage now and was living in Marina's flat.

'She told Snježana when she rang.'

The two girls were sisters and often spoke on the telephone. They were both particularly close to Marina because during the summer holidays, when Goran always tried to find families for as many of the children as possible to stay with, they and another girl called Milka had stayed with Marina for ten weeks. Crammed into her tiny flat, the four of them had got to know one another well. The girls were all in their teens and were no doubt hungry for details of Marina's tangled and to them sophisticated love life, while she in return was pleased to have some people to confide all her troubles to. At one stage the girls had been very cool towards me, seeing me as the instrument of Marina's unhappiness, which I guess was more or less true, but we all became good friends again later.

All three girls were Serbian. Milka had been abandoned by her parents when she was ten, and had no idea why. The sisters' parents had both been killed. Josipa originally had a Serbian name, Radojka, but she changed it in disgust at what her people were doing to Lipik. She also became a Roman Catholic. 'She drew a line on her past life,' Goran once told me, 'like death draws a line.'

'Do you want a coffee?' Marina asked.

'Okay.' I was coming round now and got myself dressed. We went out into the chilly darkness and walked across to the flat. It was an eerie feeling because I had no idea what to expect. I had been told about a boyfriend, but there was no sign of him in the flat. I was completely in the dark as to what had happened since I last saw Marina a month ago. We sat up all night, drinking thick, strong coffee and talking.

'I hear you have a boyfriend,' I said eventually.

'Yes.' She was watching me closely over the rim of her cup with those wonderful eyes. 'I was going to tell you.'

'Well, I already know.'

'How?'

'I'm not going to tell you.'

There was a long silence as I waited for her to elaborate, but she just smoked a cigarette and watched me, waiting for my next question. Eventually the silence of the night was too much for me.

'Is it serious?'

'Yes. He is very nice. He is very kind. He is very gentle.'

'Who is he?'

'He's called Mato.' She said no more for a moment, teasing me with her silence, then smiled and volunteered some more information. 'He is a Croatian. He read about me in a newspaper and saw my picture. He was working in Switzerland and someone sent him the paper so he would have news from home. When he saw my picture and read about me he decided that he must meet me, and so he came all the way here looking for me.'

'Just came looking for you?'

'He has a cousin, who sent him the paper. He rang the cousin and said that he would like to meet me. I knew the cousin and so he introduced us. He is a very nice boy and he loves me very much. I think that I could make a life with him.'

'That's fantastic,' I said forcefully. 'I'm very happy for you.'

I *was* happy for her, just miserable for myself. I had often told her that I could not be the right person for her. We were totally different, not just the wrong ages and the wrong nationalities, our backgrounds were so far apart we hardly understood anything about each other. We might be in love, but in my saner moments I could see that we would not be able to build a life together now that the distraction of the project was drawing to a close. Soon there would be nothing for me in Lipik. I couldn't even speak the language! My head told me all these things, but inside I felt as if I had been hit by a battering ram. Whenever I had told her in the past that she should go out and find a nice local boy her reply was

always the same, 'But I love you, I don't love anybody else.'
Now she had taken my advice and I felt wretched, not sure if
I was going to be able to handle the thought of there being
somebody else in her life.

We were still talking when dawn broke and Mato arrived,
not expecting to see Marina return until later that day. He
was even more surprised to see me, but handled it well. He
knew everything about us and our situation. He saw his role
as helping Marina to pick up the pieces of her life again, just
as I had seen myself doing fifteen months before.

Mato was still living and working in Switzerland, but his
cousin lived in a town about an hour away, so he could stay
there when he came to visit Marina. We all three sat down
and drank more coffee. It might have been easier if I had not
liked him, but I did. He was a genuine young man with a
good sense of humour and a disarming smile. I did feel
pleased for them both when I was able to think about the
situation objectively. I left them and walked back to the
hospital for a bath and a shave, having accepted an invitation
to have dinner with them and Josipa at the flat that evening.
To me it seemed like a symbolic last supper.

Marina had helped Josipa a lot since she left the orphanage,
finding her a job at the glass factory and later organizing a
flat for her in the hospital. Josipa and Mato also got on well
together, neither of them speaking much English and relying
on Marina to translate if they wanted to communicate with
me. The three of them seemed to have a lot of fun together,
babbling away in Croatian and laughing all the time. I felt
very out of it. They were a happy little family group and I
had come bursting in on them, bringing back all the memories,
the confusion and my unhappiness with me. They prepared a
very special supper with candles on the table to make the
dingy little kitchen look more attractive. I suppose I had a
little too much to drink, trying to deaden the pain, because I
became rather emotional. It seemed that I was now being
given some of my own medicine, being made to endure some

of the jealousy and unhappiness that Caroline had been going through over the previous few months.

'You know, the problem with you and me,' I remember saying to Mato, via Marina, 'is that we both have the Marina Disease.' Later in the evening I said, 'You are obviously very happy, all of you, so I am going to leave Lipik tomorrow.'

'But your flight isn't booked until next week,' Marina protested.

'I'll change it.' I was adamant. 'It is the best thing to do, the selfless thing to do. It would be selfish of me to stay. You are happy. I must leave you two to get on with your lives. I am pleased that you have found each other.'

I could see that Mato was triumphant and unable to stop himself from grinning. Whenever Marina started to cry he would jump up and gallantly dry her eyes with a tissue while I sat by helplessly and watched. 'I have been very confused,' I confessed, 'I love Marina and I also love my family. I have two boys of my own and they need a father.'

I noticed Josipa was crying and I asked what was wrong. Through Marina she said she was so happy for Edward and William because she and Snježana did not have a father and she knew what it was like.

I said goodnight to them and walked back to the orphanage. The fresh air sobered me up a little and I rang Caroline when I got there. 'I've had a very emotional evening,' I told her, 'and I'm coming back to England tomorrow.'

'Why tomorrow?'

'Because I want to get out of this place.'

'Does she really have a new boyfriend?'

'Yes.'

'You don't have to come back like this. Why are you running away? If she's got a boyfriend and they're happy, why are you running?'

'Because I can't stay here.' I was not getting the reaction I was looking for. In my arrogance I had expected her to say 'Thank goodness' and to welcome me back home.

'Well, okay, but I don't understand.'

'It's what I've decided to do and I will leave tomorrow if I can arrange a flight.'

'All right. But if you can't, don't worry, it doesn't matter.'

When I woke up I was hung over and feeling sick with unhappiness. It was a beautiful, bright, sunny morning. I walked over to the orphanage and the fresh air made me feel better. I found a pen and paper and went outside to a seat overlooking the children's playground. It was where Marina and I had sat that spring evening when I had told her that I had made my choice and I was going to stay with her in Lipik and leave Caroline.

The sun was just coming up over the trees. On the other side of the playground, with all its gleaming new equipment, the ruins of the houses along the street still stood, blackened and charred. The odd chicken and dog now stirred in the back gardens where people were beginning to rebuild their lives under sheets of corrugated iron and plastic. I remembered how bad the pot-holes had looked on the playing field; they were all gone now and the ground was beautifully relaid with a soft, gravel-like material. The seat I was sitting on was new, donated by well-wishers to replace the broken one which Marina and I had sat on eight months before. Behind the goal-posts was a still ruined bungalow-type building which I had once suggested to Marina we should buy and do up as a home. I had had a romantic image of us living out my retirement in the elegant bungalow, like retired British couples used to do in India, tending their gardens and pretending they were back in England. I could see us starting a young family of our own, with the children from the orphanage dropping in for tea on the lawn on warm summer afternoons. It was a vision which Marina had dismissed with a shrug, a dream that had not made it across the gap in our ages and our cultures.

I took out pen and paper and began to write my farewell letter to her. I told her how happy I was for her and Mato, that we had achieved what we had set out to do and created a beautiful home for the children. I thanked her for her love and wished her every happiness for the future, hoping that we could always be friends. Sealing the letter into an envelope, I went into the orphanage and rang Croatian Airlines. I managed to reserve a ticket on the midday flight out of Zagreb, which meant I had to leave quickly. I rang Marina at the flat and asked if she and Mato could take me to the airport. Mato rushed off to get some petrol for the car and arrived back a little later. Marina was driving, with Mato and Josipa sitting in the back, giggling and playing cards. The poor little Yugo could hardly move under the weight of us all as Marina ground the gears and revved the engine mercilessly.

The car went so slowly, with Marina seldom bothering to change out of third gear, that I was becoming increasingly nervous about making the flight on time. I could not imagine what I would do if I missed the plane because the other three had arranged to go into Zagreb together for a 'family' day out and I certainly did not want to be tagging along. As we rattled and groaned down the almost deserted motorway at about sixty miles an hour there was suddenly a juddering crash and a rhythmic drumbeat of disaster from somewhere under the car. 'I think we had better stop,' I said as calmly as I could, and the drumbeat slowed to silence as we pulled into the side of the road and viewed the shredded front tyre and the wheel rim resting on the tarmac.

Looking at my watch, I saw we had half an hour until take-off and now I was truly desperate. Everything came out of the boot in the search for the spare tyre. Marina wandered up and down the road, smoking, while Mato, who was obviously as keen as I was that I should get on that plane, and I worked feverishly. I doubt if we could have gone any faster had we been in a Formula One pit stop. Spanners flew everywhere as we tried to shift the rusted wheelnuts. One of the nuts gave up and broke in the spanner and eventually we managed to wrest the others off and put on the almost bald spare tyre. We got going again with only twenty minutes left to take-off and I had not even got my ticket.

We reached the terminal and I ran inside, bought the ticket and checked my bags in, by which time the other three had parked the car and come in to say goodbye. There was no time to hang around, I had to go straight through. I kissed Josipa, giving her a little gift of some money, and shook hands with Mato. I kissed Marina and gave her the letter, saying, 'Read this when I've gone.' I walked through to the plane, which was waiting to take off, and headed back to England. I glanced back only once and saw them walking off, Mato with his arm round Marina's shoulders.

Caroline met me at the other end and drove me home. She was obviously pleased it was over, but she wished it had been because I wanted it that way, not because Marina had found another boyfriend. Clearly my love was not dead, I had simply been squeezed out.

The following day, Monday, I rang Marina to say that I had arrived safely.

'Oh, good.' She sounded light and cheery.

'Did you have a good day yesterday?'

'Yes, it was good. We went to the zoo and bought some ice creams. It was lovely.'

The following day I rang her again. 'How are you?'

'Good.'

'How are things?'

'They are good.'

'Marina, just tell me one thing. Do you really love Mato?'

There was a long pause at the other end. 'There is only one person I love, and that is you.' There was another long silence. 'You must know that.'

I felt a tremendous surge of emotion. What on earth was I going to do now? Later in the day Caroline and I were sitting down to a meal. 'You were right,' I confessed, 'I made a big mistake rushing away like that. I didn't finish my business down there. We haven't sorted out about the furniture or anything. I've got to go back.'

'All right.' She sighed.

19

One Day at a Time

Now I was lying endlessly to Caroline on the pretext of protecting her from hurt, and to Marina for the same reason. In reality I was lying because I was frightened to tell either of them the truth. What I wanted more than anything else was a peaceful life, but I had completely messed that up. I still did not want to lose either of them, but deep inside I knew that I couldn't get away with that. I had to choose, but I could not find the strength to do it, not yet. I kept postponing any kind of decision and continued to tell lies and to cover up the truth, just to get myself from one day to the next. I was being selfish and weak and I felt deeply guilty and ashamed of myself.

Poor Goran was summoned back to Zagreb airport to pick me up once again, which he did with his usual unquestioning kindness and patience. 'Marina said she would like you to see her after supper, for coffee,' he told me as we drove back down the same road I had travelled so miserably a few days before. Goran's English, which had been very sparse when I first met him, had come on tremendously in the fifteen months of the project and we could now talk easily to one another.

I had a pleasant supper with him and his family, half dreading what was coming and at the same time wishing the minutes would pass so that I could make a polite exit and go to Marina's flat. I was desperate to see her, but uncomfortable at the thought of barging into their tight little family group again. Eventually the meal was over and I bade Goran and Gordana goodnight, walking down the silent, dark and deserted road to Marina's block, under the looming shadows of the shattered houses. When I got there she answered the door

189

herself and Snoopy came yapping and leaping out to greet me. There was no sign of Mato.

'Where is Mato?' I asked, trying to sound as if I was making casual conversation.

'He has gone away for a week, to give us time to talk and decide.' I was surprised and impressed yet again by Mato's maturity and understanding. Once more Marina and I talked long into the night, going over much the same territory we had been over dozens of times before but unable to resist raking it all up again.

'Tomorrow we are doing a radio bridge to New York,' she told me at one stage. 'You must come too.'

'A radio bridge?'

'A broadcast to a Croatian radio programme in New York. I have arranged it to raise money over there.'

'That sounds great.'

This gave us something to focus on, a way of resuming our lives together as we returned to the cause of raising money and telling the story of Lipik to the world, a distraction from our own self-absorption.

The following day Marina, Josipa, Goran, the builder, Marino the Mayor and I all went to Daruvar, where the broadcast was to take place, and spent the evening there. The broadcast was being conducted over a telephone link, which was plagued by last-minute hitches and broken lines. When we finally got through, we each described what we were doing in Lipik and what still needed to be done. Then Croatians in New York phoned in pledging money for the cause. It was an exciting night and helped to get me back into my life in Croatia.

On the plane down I was travelling with a group of pilgrims on their way to Medjugorje in southern Croatia, a village where two young girls had had a vision of the Virgin Mary. I started talking to them and as we were coming in to land I asked them if they would pray for the children and the orphanage. They promised they would do so at a special time when they believed that their prayers would be answered.

I forgot about the promise until a letter arrived for Marina containing a cheque from the pastor in Medjugorje. It had been posted on the day that I had caught the flight down.

Eighteen months earlier an artist had come to see us when the news of the project first broke. 'I heard what you are doing,' he told me, 'and I would like you to have a complete set of prints of my work.'

They were lovely, large, colourful pictures. 'They're perfect,' I said, 'we shall hang them in the orphanage when it is finished.'

'No, no,' he interrupted, 'you misunderstand. These are for you. When the orphanage is finished I will give you another set for the walls here.'

So that week Marina and I drove to his house in the remote wooded hills to collect them. There was thick snow on the ground and more falling from the sky as the tired, rusty little Yugo puffed its way through the dramatic black and white forests. We stayed for lunch and he gave us about thirty pictures which we took back to get framed.

One afternoon, Goran and I were asked to go to a meeting in Zagreb with the Minister of Labour and Social Welfare, Mr Ivan Parać. When we got there we were shown into a very smart waiting room and I was surprised to find that there were TV cameras and newspaper reporters there too, but no one would tell me why. Eventually the minister arrived, well after the appointed time, and there was obviously some confusion and embarrassment. The minister made a nice speech about what I had done, and thanked me for it, and then presented me with a ceramic plaque of Zagreb and a beautiful book about Croatia.

'And what,' he asked, 'do you think the new home should be called?'

The people of Lipik had already decided that it would be called after me, so I was slightly taken aback by his question.

'I have not thought about it,' I replied. 'For me the name is not really important.'

He asked me to let him know if I came up with an idea, and then we moved into his large, grand office for a general and informal discussion away from the media.

On our way back in the car I asked Goran about the confusion over the name. He was overcome with embarrassment as he drove out of Zagreb. It transpired that it had been intended that the minister should announce to me, in the presence of the press, that it was going to be called the Mark Cook Children's Home. Just before the meeting he was informed by the Government's legal advisers that this was not possible, as I was still alive. I assured Goran that I did not think the name was worth dying for.

I had been asked by BBC Radio to appear in London the following Wednesday on *Midweek*, introduced by Libby Purves, the well-known broadcaster and journalist. The programme format has a few people sitting round a table with her, chatting about what they are doing. It is a popular programme with a large audience, as I was to find out later. My participation had been organized by the young couple from Fortesque's who were putting on the ball for us, on the understanding that at some time in the interview I would mention the event. I felt I owed it to them to do it, and as we also still needed a lot of money, this was an excellent opportunity to talk to a big audience. I flew back to England again on the Tuesday. By this stage Marina and I had realized that we wanted to be together more than anything else. While I was away in England, Marina was going to tell Mato that we had reached a decision and that it was over between them. I was supposed to tell Caroline as well.

The ball organizers had managed to persuade the Conrad Hotel, a fabulously luxurious establishment overlooking Chelsea Harbour in London, to put us up at no charge for the night before the interview. Caroline met me and we headed for London and our suite overlooking the Thames. I found the culture shock of being amidst the rubble of Lipik in the morning and wallowing in all this luxury in the evening very troubling. I did not like the idea that we were enjoying a dinner which was costing more than someone like Marina would earn in a month. I felt very uncomfortable and out of my element. It was a very sticky evening.

The car arrived in the morning and whisked me up to the BBC building above Oxford Circus. It was a most enjoyable experience. Libby Purves was very relaxed, sitting on the floor in the hospitality suite before we went in, chatting to me and the other guests, and then wandering into the studio just before the show was due to start and continuing the conversation in front of the microphones. It must have gone well because I received a great deal of feedback afterwards. At one stage in the chat Libby Purves asked what I planned to do next, once the orphanage was finished.

'I don't know,' I confessed. 'I will be looking for something else to get my teeth into.'

That casual comment resulted in an avalanche of offers from people looking for someone to raise funds for them. I was amazed by the variety of good causes all out looking for money, but none of them struck me as the thing I really wanted to do next. Unfortunately, the programme did not raise enough interest in the Lipik Ball to save it, and it had to be cancelled a few days later, which meant that the young couple who had tried so hard to get it going ended up losing money, which was very bad luck. At the same time, I have to admit, I was rather relieved that we were not going to have to cope with a formal event just at that moment.

On the way home to Wiltshire from London, Caroline and I stopped at a prep school where I gave another talk, which raised £700. But I was wandering around in a daze, working on automatic pilot. I had told the story of Lipik so often by then that it did not require much effort to keep doing it while my mind tried to sort out what was happening on the personal side of my life, with no success at all. I was feeling desperately guilty about the hell I had been putting Caroline through, especially now that I knew I was going to make it even worse.

I was completely unable to make any decisions more than a day in advance. I was in England for a week and did not pluck up the courage to tell Caroline that Mato had gone, kidding myself that I was keeping quiet to protect her, when in fact I was just protecting myself. As long as Caroline believed that Mato was in Lipik she could tolerate the idea of my going down there until the job was finished. As soon as she discovered the truth, we would be back into a situation of irreconcilable differences and confrontation, and, in my cowardice, I wanted to avoid that for as long as possible.

So many of my views had changed since leaving the army. For nearly forty-five years, since going away to prep school at six, I had followed rules without question, actually believing that it mattered what I wore and how I behaved in certain situations. Suddenly all that had been stripped away. I had got to know people with whom I would never have been able to mix if I had stayed in the safe tramlines of my old life; they had opened my eyes and stripped away all the comfortable old certainties. My awakening might have landed me in a mess, and perhaps part of the mess was caused by my own naivety and lack of experience in the world outside the army, but it had also broadened my horizons and changed my perspective, leaving me confused but in many ways enriched.

While I was in England we went to the Remembrance Sunday service in Wylye church. My experiences in Croatia had made me even more aware of the sacrifices which people have made down the centuries in defence of their countries' freedom. I knew that all the members of our local branch of the British Legion would be marching up and down in their bowler hats and medals. I could not help but think of the heroism and suffering of people like Jura, Marino the Mayor and Marina, who had fought so bravely to defend their town and their families, and I wanted to remember them in my own quiet way.

We deliberately arrived at the last moment before the

service was due to begin. As we got to the door all the old bemedalled comrades were formed up on parade with the general at their head. As I walked past, one of them shouted out, 'Why aren't you on parade, Cook?'

'I've had enough of that,' I said. 'I've left the army now.' I felt a great sense of guilt at letting down these people who had expected certain things of me when I moved into their village and had perhaps been disappointed by my attitude. Perhaps I was doomed to disappoint everybody.

Caroline could see that I was upset and on edge all through that time at home and assumed that it was because of Mato. She felt bad that the affair had not ended as she would have chosen, but she was working hard at coming to terms with that. More than anything she wanted to come out to see the finished orphanage. I really wanted her to see it because I was terribly proud of it and wanted to show her everything we had achieved. She had worked so hard on the administration in England and she more than deserved to be part of the final success. She had answered phones and faxes, written letters, banked money and sent information round the world, dealt with inquiries and helped me with my lectures. She had also been forced to suffer all the embarrassment and humiliation of having her private hurt displayed on the front pages of the *Daily Express*. She had done all that despite the fact that she had known I was building the orphanage for Marina as well as for the children. Had she chosen to reject the whole project, we would have been set back very badly. I could not imagine what would happen if Caroline and Marina met now in Lipik, but I seemed unable to make any decisions on the subject. She wanted to go out, I wanted her to see the orphanage, and I did not have the courage to say that it could not happen.

In the end we decided on a plan which I told myself might just work. When Dan's Van went down to Lipik, Caroline would go with it as one of the passengers, along with the reporter and photographers who were organizing the trip.

The idea was that the van would be there in time for the children's return, so there would be a double opportunity for publicity, on the van's departure from England and on the return of the children. It was decided that the children would return on Friday, 10 December, and Caroline would be in Lipik for that. I had this image in my mind of Dan's Van arriving just after the children with Father Christmas and lots of presents inside.

The return of the children was growing into quite a media event. The BBC was keen to cover it, following George Eykyn's reports on Breakfast News. I was rather hoping that Martin Bell would be able to do this as the story almost started with him and he had been so helpful, but I was told he was busy in America. There was controversy at the time about there not being enough 'good news' on TV news programmes and so I stressed to the BBC that here was an opportunity for a wonderful 'good news' feature. Meanwhile, Michael Nicholson heard about the story and rang me to say he would like to be there as well to report it for ITN. He had a special association with this sort of project because he had just published a book called *Natasha's Story* about his experiences in taking a little girl from the bombed orphanage in Sarajevo. So the two major news networks were going to be covering the event simultaneously, which gave it considerable status in the eyes of the rest of the media.

I flew out on Saturday, 4 December. Caroline drove to London the same day to meet up with the other people who were going to be travelling out in the van, and they set off overland. I believed that if she arrived close to the day of the children's return there would be so much going on that there would not be time for us to become introspective or for a confrontation to develop between Caroline and Marina. At that stage the Lipik Ball was still due to take place and so I imagined that Caroline and I would be flying back to England together for it, once the children were reinstated in their home. This confusion of mixed motives and half-baked efforts to make amends is the closest I came to having any kind of plan.

20

The Worst Nightmares

Some weeks before, the Nationwide Building Society had contacted me to say that they wanted to send some toys down in Dan's Van, and to present a cheque. So it was arranged that the van would go to their headquarters first, where there were dancers, music, balloons and all the razzamatazz. Teddy bears would be loaded into the back of the van and the newspapers would take photographs. Caroline went along to do all that and gave the media some interviews.

I had decided that I wanted to get lots of pictures up on the walls of the orphanage by the time the children arrived, because at the moment everything in the buildings was brilliant white and pristine, but rather clinical. I wanted it to be more friendly and homely. We had the prints from the Croatian artist, plus hundreds of superb photographs, so while I was in England I bought boxes of clip-frames, which weighed a ton. There must have been nearly a hundred frames.

The station manager of Croatian Airlines at Heathrow, Mr Slobodan Urlić, who knew me pretty well by now, having first become aware of my activities when he saw *Hearts of Gold*, always let me take excess baggage whenever I had things for the orphanage. The next time I was at the airport following the TV show, I had 300 calendars with me to give to the builders and architects. They had been delivered direct to the airport by Howitts Calendars, the amazingly efficient firm who put the project together for the BBC. It was not until I actually arrived for the flight that I realized just how big a pile it would be. That was when the airline first came to my rescue. They were also very understanding on a later trip when Goran asked me to buy enough English grass seed to cover the 2,000 or so square metres of bald earth which still surrounded the buildings. I imagined that I would be able to unload the boxes of frames straight from the baggage carousel at Zagreb on to a trolley and out to Goran's waiting car, as I had with the calendars. I did not envisage any real problems, even though there was far more than I could possibly carry on my own.

When I got to the airport they told us that the plane was still at Zagreb because the airport was fog-bound. We waited in the departure lounge for several hours before we received any news, impatiently walking around the duty-free areas and drinking endless cups of coffee. At four in the afternoon we were told that the plane would not be able to fly from Zagreb that day, so our flight back would be cancelled. I felt desperate. I really wanted to get back to Lipik and to Marina. The delay was almost intolerable.

'There is another plane going to Slovenia,' they told me, 'to Ljubjana airport. You could go on that one.'

'Yes, please, anything,' I agreed, and they switched all the baggage over to the new flight.

I could not expect Goran to trail out to meet me now, so I rang Marina and told her what was happening, before having to dash to the plane. She said she would go to Zagreb and wait for news of my arrival. She gave me a telephone number she would be at, which I stuffed into my pocket.

Ljubjana is about seventy miles from Zagreb and we arrived in the middle of the night. It was freezing cold and there was no transport available anywhere. After a long wait a bus showed up and I loaded all my boxes into it, as did several other people in a similar position to me, including an American businessman who was out there to give Christmas gifts to business contacts and was particularly helpful.

The bus took us into the town, where they told us we could get a train to Zagreb. It did not actually go to the station, however, but dumped us in the street, in the snow, about 300 yards away. That doesn't sound like much of a distance, until you start trying to shift boxes full of glass frames, on your own, with no trolley. I could hardly ask the American to help, since he had luggage of his own. The train was due in half an hour. I staggered backwards and forwards with these boxes, my knees buckling under the weight of them, barely able to pick them up. The ticket office would only accept Slovenian dollars, so I asked the American if he would mind changing money and buying the tickets while I continued to drag the boxes in from the snow.

'I've got the tickets,' he said as I came in with the last box, 'it's platform number six.'

'Where's that?' It was an enormous rail terminal and in the fog it was hard to see more than a few yards. Number six was the furthest possible platform, about 200 yards across numerous railway lines. The American went on ahead and I started ferrying the boxes again. By now I hated them with a vengeance but I was determined not to let them beat me. The pile on the platform slowly grew as the one in the ticket office shrank. I had one box left in the ticket office when I heard the train in the distance and a light appeared out of the fog. We had been told that it would not be stopping for long, just long enough to let people on and off. With every muscle in my body screaming with agony, I ran back across the lines for the last box, hauled it back and loaded it on to the train with the others. Looking around I couldn't see my cases, which I thought the American had said he would bring. 'Where are my cases?' I screamed with the little breath I had left.

'Gee, I don't know. Did you leave them at the ticket office?'

'Don't let them go!' I shouted over my shoulder as I headed back to the ticket office. The train was emitting angry noises and people were shouting by the time I got back and threw the cases in ahead of me. It was a freezing night but I was in a muck-sweat, my chest heaving for breath and my heart pounding in my ears. I collapsed in a heap, certain that this was my punishment for everything I had done wrong in the last few months. I must have been closer to a heart attack than at any time in my life, and I began seriously to question my sanity. I hauled a duty-free bottle of whisky out of my case, unscrewed the cap and had a very large dram.

We arrived in Zagreb at about one in the morning and I discovered I had lost Marina's telephone number. I rang Goran, getting him out of bed, and asked where she was. He gave me the Zagreb number, which I rang, and she came round in the car with Josipa to rescue me. How we managed to get all the boxes in around Josipa I do not know, but we did it somehow. With Josipa sitting with her face squashed against the window and her knees up under her chin, we drove slowly to Lipik through the fog and snow – one of the headlights still didn't work too well. Fortunately the police all seemed to have gone to bed and the Jordanian soldiers at the UN checkpoint sent us through with a cheery wave despite the snow. By the time we got to the orphanage it was almost dawn.

The furniture was arriving and being erected all over the buildings that week, and I was busy putting pictures up on the walls. Snoopy scuttled around my feet on the shiny new tiled floors.

Meanwhile, Dan's Van was trundling across Europe with Caroline, Tom Thirkell the organizer, two freelance photographers and a freelance reporter called Simon Worrell who was supposedly writing a nice feature for the *Daily Express*. He had a bulky, very old-fashioned-looking tape-recorder with him which he kept thrusting towards Caroline whenever she spoke. They were all friends of Dan's who were heavily involved in the memorial project with his mother, Kathy. There was little communication from them as they meandered their way down through Europe from hotel to hotel. As they also broke down in Zagreb, which added another night to the journey, they did not actually arrive in Lipik until Thursday, about eleven o'clock in the morning, after five days' travelling. As Caroline got out of the car I embraced her to the sound of clicking cameras. I could tell she was on edge and assumed it was because she could sense that I was ill at ease. The others all wanted a guided tour of the area and I had arranged for a charming Indian gentleman from the UN, Mr Kishore Mandhyan, to take them around.

'You really should go as well,' I told Caroline. 'It's very interesting. He's going to take them to all sorts of places you wouldn't get to without a UN vehicle.'

'Are you sure?' She looked doubtful. 'Wouldn't you like me to stay here with you and look round the orphanage?'

'No, you go ahead,' I assured her. 'We'll do all that when you return.'

They arrived back about six o'clock after a very interesting and almost fatal day. At one stage, led by an Argentinian officer, they were walking up to a Serbian gun position, when their guide suddenly stopped in his tracks; there, one pace ahead of him, was a wire at ankle-height connected to a booby-trap mine. Had it not been for his vigilance there is no doubt that one of them would have set it off.

After much-needed drinks, I suggested that we should do a guided tour around the orphanage for everyone. 'I don't want to go with everyone else,' Caroline insisted. 'I want you to show me round on my own.'

'Are you sure?' I blundered on. 'Wouldn't it be better to do it all in one go?'

'Please, please' – I could see the desperation in her face now – 'please will you show me round the orphanage on our own?'

So we left the others and went off together. Clearly I was not behaving normally and the atmosphere was horribly strained. I simply could not get the right tone and did the tour as I would have done if she had been with a group of foreign tourists. This was not how she had been hoping it would be as she crossed Europe, being constantly interviewed and having a microphone pushed under her face by Simon Worrell every time she opened her mouth. When we finally got down to the cellars and I was showing her all the boilers and pipework, she stopped. 'What's wrong?' she asked.

'What do you mean?' I avoided her eyes.

'I mean, what's happened? There's something wrong, isn't there? Is Mato still here?'

'No.'

'Oh, my God. What's happened?'

I proceeded to tell her the story, standing in the same cellars that the children had been forced to live in all those months ago. It could not have been a worse or crueller time and place in which to tell her all this. Once again I had mismanaged everything to the most incredible degree and I now had no idea what to do for the best.

'Are you leaving me?' she asked eventually.

'Yes.'

We continued to talk in the cellar as all the others went over to Number Two for supper. It was obvious to them all that something had happened. Nicky, one of the photographers who had grown quite close to Caroline on the trip down, saw her crying, and tried to comfort both of us before going off with the others. When they had all gone and the buildings were quiet, Caroline and I went over to the kitchen block and found some pieces of bread to munch on before going back to the hospital where we were staying. The others were all staying in the orphanage, so we would at least get some privacy there. We drank a lot of whisky and yet again talked long into the night, with great emotion, total despair and misery.

The following day the children were due, with all the media in tow, and it should have been one of the happiest days of our lives. I had arranged that the children should arrive by one o'clock so that the television crews could get their stories in time to send them back to England for the evening news bulletins.

'I can't face this,' Caroline announced. 'I'm going to Zagreb. It's better if I'm not here.'

'You can't do that. How will you get there?'

'I'll hitch a lift. I'll do anything. I've got to get out.'

I tried every way possible to get her a lift to Zagreb but no one in Lipik was leaving that day. The thought of Caroline standing by the side of the road with her bags, trying to hitch a lift, was unbearable. The others were now becoming involved in the situation. They had been going back and forth to Number Two for breakfast and it was then that we discovered Simon Worrell had been on the phone in the café, calling the *Daily Express* in London, giving them a blow-by-blow account of our personal nightmare which we were conveniently unfolding in front of him. Imagining that we were among sympathetic friends, we had allowed our guards to drop. It seemed that Caroline and I had still not learnt our lesson with the tabloid media.

I went storming into the café where Simon was sitting and called him names that I don't think I have ever used to anyone before. I truly wanted to kill him. I stormed out before I could inflict any physical damage on him. He had befriended Caroline and then betrayed her. His excuse was that if the *Daily Express* had found out and he had missed the story they would never have used him again. He had told them that Caroline was trying to hitch a lift to Zagreb having left me, and hearing it told like that made Caroline think again, giving her something to fight against. She went over to confront him.

'What do you mean?' she demanded. 'I haven't left my husband. I'm not going to Zagreb, I'm staying here. What do you mean? What have you done? You will retract that story immediately because it's a pack of lies. If you don't I'll ring them myself.'

'Okay.' He stood up. 'I'll ring them back and tell them it isn't as I thought and tell them to hold the story.'

We all continued to wait for the return of the children.

21

The Return of the Children

Martin Bell's face popped round the office door as I sat lost in thought. 'Hi.'

'Hallo!' I jumped up in surprise. I was so pleased to see him. 'I didn't think you would be able to make it. They said you were in America.'

'I was, but I've come back for this.'

'That's great.'

A few minutes later Michael Nicholson and his ITN team turned up and Caroline and I were able to distract ourselves with small-talk as we hung around waiting for the children to appear. There was obviously a long-standing and friendly rivalry between the two newsmen. 'When that man leaves,' Martin called across to me while I was talking to Michael, 'count your children. He steals them from places like this.'

I took Michael in to show him around the building and he was clearly amazed by the quality of the workmanship and the standard of the accommodation. As we wandered round one of the huge, spanking-new apartments he turned to me and said, 'This is wonderful. You do know both my parents are dead, don't you?'

The weather was perfect, still cold, with some snow hanging around on the ground, but bright sunshine. As I tried to be chatty and cheerful I could hear my own voice echoing in my ears and I knew that I was acting strangely. 'Could I have a word in private?' I said to Martin eventually and steered him away to one side. 'I think I have to tell you that things have all gone horribly wrong down here today for me personally. What should have been one of the happiest days of my life has turned out to be a traumatic disaster.' I went on to outline the problem to him. 'I thought I must explain the situation to you in case you think Caroline and I are behaving strangely. Please, I would be so grateful if you don't say anything about this in your report.'

'God, no.' He was shocked at the very suggestion. 'I'm out here to cover the return of the children. I understand your situation completely, I've been through the odd personal crisis myself. Don't worry, I know all the problems.'

I was very grateful to him for his understanding. 'Do you think I should tell Michael Nicholson?' I asked.

'Don't worry, I'll explain it to him.'

As we continued to wait I noticed that Simon Worrell, whom I had been pointedly ignoring up to then, was not looking well. Several of the others went to his rescue as he appeared to be on the point of collapse with a violent fever. Nicky came over to me. 'I think he's really quite ill,' she said, 'we've got to get him to a doctor.' I looked across and saw that he looked very puffed up and appeared to be in great distress, becoming delirious.

'Go round the back there' – I pointed into the park – 'follow the path along to the hospital and you'll see a sign for Ambulance. That is the doctor's surgery.' They disappeared round the corner as the bus finally pulled up in front of the buildings, the doors opened and the children spilled off, led by Vladek and Stanko. I went over to greet and embrace them all, one by one, as they got off the bus. It was the fulfilment of my dream, the moment I had been working towards for eighteen months, and I was choked with emotion when Martin tried to interview me. Darinka, a teacher who had worked for thirty years at the orphanage, whose own home had been destroyed, and who had been down in Selce with the children, had also come back with them. Tears were streaming down her cheeks as she got out of the bus and looked around the wreckage of her home town and then up for the first time at the pretty pink palace we had built for the children in the midst of it all.

'Where's Marina?' I asked Goran quietly in the middle of all these emotional scenes.

'I don't know.' He looked around, puzzled. 'I haven't seen her.'

Earlier I had said to Marina that I hoped she would be there for the arrival of the children, since it was the moment we had been working for ever since I made the promise by her hospital bed. But I knew that it was going to be very difficult for her with Caroline standing in the background, and she rather resented what she saw as a British media circus.

We took the children into the main block and up the staircase to the playroom at the top, keeping them there while we brought Dan's Van with Father Christmas out of its hiding place and parked it in the quadrangle between the buildings. While everyone was milling around in the playroom Marino the Mayor arrived with Marina, and Caroline kept discreetly in the background, but there were enough people around to cover up any difficulties. We then brought the children down for their presents, which Father Christmas handed out from the back of the van. Lunch was being cooked in the kitchen, the television crews did their interviews, leaving hurriedly to make their deadlines, and the 'good news' was seen by millions of people that night on both BBC and ITV.

Caroline had brought out some wonderful little cuddly toys, all dressed in Christmas hats and scarves, and some tartan rugs which had been donated. She and I went round the bedrooms in the afternoon, putting them on each of the children's beds for their first night home. We wanted them to feel completely comfortable and to know that there were people who loved them and wanted them there in Lipik. I had systematically been having brass plaques made with the names of major donors and people who had been particularly helpful to our cause, and so each of the rooms had one of these names by the door, giving it a little bit more individuality.

Helping to put the children to bed, it was agonizing for me to watch Caroline as she went round the rooms talking, playing and cuddling the children. She was totally at home with them and they responded to her love and natural motherly instincts. 'I feel so sad,' she said when we had finished the job, 'to think that I won't be seeing any of these children again. I hardly know them but I love them already.'

The next morning I drove Dan's Van to the airport with Caroline sitting in the front with me. The others sat quietly in the back. We all made half-hearted efforts to be merry and I was amazed once again by Caroline's strength and the way she controlled herself and put on a brave face. At the airport I said goodbye to the others, ignoring Simon, and kissed Caroline. She turned and went through passport control. It seemed as if I had finally made a decision and a choice. I was going to start a new life and I still felt miserable. I just knew that I could not possibly have said hallo to the children one day and goodbye the next. I had built the home for them and I wanted to share their excitement in settling back into it, including having Christmas with them.

When I got back to Lipik I went to see Marina, who was on duty at the Ambulance in Pakrac. She could not believe it when I walked through the door and her eyes sparkled like diamonds. She had convinced herself that I would get on the plane back to England with Caroline.

'Where were you when the children arrived yesterday?' I asked later on. 'I was so sad that you missed it.'

'I wasn't invited. Goran did not bother to invite me.'

'You didn't need an invitation.' I couldn't believe what I was hearing. 'He didn't invite me either. Did you expect a formal invitation?'

She ignored me. 'He didn't even invite Marino. Marino saw the bus going past his office window and telephoned me. I said I hadn't been invited either. He said, "You're coming with me." He came and collected me from the hospital.' She pouted and flared her eyes simultaneously.

'Well, I think you were silly not to come if that was all that was worrying you.' I was annoyed that she had missed such an important moment by taking a stand.

She shrugged and was quiet for a moment, then began again. 'The children said to me, when I saw them, "Where were you? We looked for you. It was you we wanted to see and you weren't there." I told them, "I wasn't invited."' She gave another violent shrug and lit a cigarette.

I decided that it was time to change the subject. 'Were you at the Ambulance when they brought that reporter from the *Daily Express* round?'

'He was from the *Daily Express*?'

'Yes.'

'I didn't know. I knew he was a reporter. I said to him, "Do you know who I am?" He said, "Yes." I wondered why he looked so scared.' She laughed. 'I gave him four big injections. I am glad.' The irony of the situation was not lost on either of us.

At last, Marina felt, she was able to get a little of her own back against the newspaper that had caused her so much pain and shattered her dreams. Some months earlier Annie Leask had rung her from Zagreb to ask if she could visit the orphanage and, after discussing it with the Mayor, Marina told her that her safety in Lipik could not be guaranteed.

When Caroline reached Heathrow there were photographers waiting for her, alerted by Simon, and a reporter from the *News of the World*. When I spoke to Kathy Eldon later to thank her for the Land-Rover she told me that Nicky, the photographer, who we had thought was the only one on our side, had called the *News of the World* from Lipik. The reporter was sent to the airport to get a statement from Caroline and followed her on to the underground train back into London, pestering her for comments. Caroline remained silent.

The *Daily Express* made Simon's story front-page news yet again and ran it over three days, ruthlessly misquoting remarks which Caroline had inadvertently made on the way down in the van, believing that she was among friends and people who wanted to help.

22

Built with Love, for Love

Five days later, when we held the official opening, the last of the snow had melted away. Over 200 people were expected for the ceremony at eleven o'clock in the morning, including the Minister for Social Welfare from Zagreb and His Excellency Mr Bryan Sparrow, the British Ambassador. Hordes of police arrived first to check on security.

We all made speeches. Bryan Sparrow said many kind things and ended by saying, 'The result of Colonel Cook's efforts is that the home is restored, the children are back where they belong and Lipik has begun its slow and sure return to normality. Let this story shine like a bright light in dark and tragic times, so that all can strive to end the present troubles and be inspired to rebuild their lives and communities.'

I was very aware that Marina had not received as much credit as she should have for being the inspiration behind the project. Because her time in recent months had been taken up with her work at the hospital and in politics, most of the day-to-day business had fallen to Goran and me, and to Ivan during the building stage. Because I had been cautious about pushing Marina forward to the media and to British visitors like the ambassador, few knew about our relationship and many of the people there assumed that Goran had been the inspiration behind the project rather than her. I wanted to set the record straight in my own speech, which had to be translated as I went along.

'Eighteen months ago, Dr Topić and I had a dream to rebuild this home. Today that dream has come true. But for me the home is much better than the dream. Outside you can see that it is beautiful. Inside it is fantastic, but more importantly it has a feeling of warmth and love. There are many people to thank,' and I listed the builders and the architects and all the people around the world who had supported us. 'This home is beautiful and a symbol of hope for the future. Most importantly, it is a home for eighty children. It is a loving home for any child of any race or any creed. In this terrible situation the children are the innocent victims and I would like to address them now directly.'

Many of the children were standing near me in the choir as I turned to talk to them. 'This is your home, be proud of your home, it is one of the nicest in Croatia. Many people will come and visit you while you are here. Remember you are the hosts. Enjoy living here and I hope you will be very happy and live together in peace and in love.' I then thanked particularly Goran, for his role in saving the children in the first place and working so hard with me on the reconstruction, and Marino the Mayor who, despite all the problems he had to handle, was always courteous and understanding and had time for everybody. 'Finally I would like to thank my very special friend, Dr Marina Topić. It was her idea to rebuild the home. If she had not had this dream and shared it with me it would today still be a ruin. Together we have built this home.' I ended by saying, in Croatian, '*Izgradio sam ovaj dom s ljubavu i za ljubav* – I have built this house with love, for love.'

One of the local dignitaries also made a speech in Croatian and I could see that his words were pleasing Marina. 'What did he say?' I asked her.

'He said that if Colonel Cook has been the bricks and the mortar for this project, Dr Topić has been the cement which has kept it together.'

It is always hard to ensure that everyone is thanked as fully as they should be at events like this, without the speeches becoming too long and tedious. It is even harder when two languages are involved. A number of people from the UN

Protection Force were there, and Hugo Anson, a good friend and Head of Civil Affairs, came up to me afterwards, saddened that no mention had been made of their presence in the area, without which it would not have been possible to do anything in Lipik. As they pointed out to me, more orphans were being created all over the world by the deaths of UN soldiers serving in Croatia. The Acting Sector Commander, Colonel Evergisto de Vergara from Argentina, wrote me a moving letter afterwards, congratulating me and then pointing out the role of UNPROFOR. He ended: 'In the last two days my home country, Argentina, added another three orphans to its list. Captain Rojas lost his life while he was in the service of peace 15,000 miles away from his family when his car hit an anti-tank mine. First Sergeant Balla lost his legs and, God willing, we don't have to add another four orphans to that list. It is good to remember that before UNPROFOR came to this area, Lipik was a ghost town.'

Mladen Grbin was also upset that I had not thanked SOS for Children. I was not sure how I could have done that, since I saw myself as being part of the organization and it would have been like thanking myself. But it showed me just how sensitive people can be about having their efforts appreciated and I was sorry to upset him because he had been so helpful to me as a sounding-board for ideas, full of useful advice on legal and financial matters. He came out several times to see how we were progressing, and everything would have been a great deal more difficult without his efforts.

I am sure that there will be other people I met during this period of my life who will feel disappointed that I have not included them in this narrative. I can only apologize and fall back on the excuse that there were just so many people who were kind and helpful in so many ways that it would be impossible to include them all without producing a book consisting of little more than a list of names.

Towards the end of the ceremony there was the cutting of the ribbon across the door, which was done by Vladek and the minister under the eye of the Croatian television cameras. Vladek then sliced the ribbon up into pieces which were presented to various people as souvenirs. Bouquets of flowers were given out and then we went back to our seats as the elderly local priest said prayers. The ceremony ended with songs and dances performed by groups of local children. Towards the end they started singing in English, performing the lovely spiritual, 'Nobody knows the troubles I've seen . . .' Then they turned, looked directly at me and sang, 'Somebody loves me, I don't know who . . .' It was beautiful and I was deeply moved.

Food and drinks were laid out in the playroom at the top of the main building, so that everyone could walk up through the apartments and see the work for themselves before gathering in the room at the top to socialize.

I took Marino the Mayor aside and pointed at one of the photographs I had put up on the walls. It showed him with Marina and me in the ruins of the kitchen, beneath the clock with the hands stuck at 5.32 when the shelling started. It was taken on the day of our first meeting and Marino had a bored expression on his face. You could almost see a bubble coming out of his head saying, 'Promises, promises.'

'Mark,' he said, his face wreathed in smiles. 'Mark,' he patted me on the arm, 'I will be honest with you. When you first came to me with this promise to rebuild the orphanage, I didn't believe you would ever do it. I thought you were like everyone else who comes here and makes wild promises, and you would forget about us as soon as you went away and the memory faded. I never thought you would succeed, never.'

Ros Hardie and Caro Brewster had flown out from Scotland with Mladen Grbin, and another kind couple who had raised a lot of money for us, Colin and Delia Bolden, drove all the way out from England to be there at the opening. That night we went on to have another party in the dining room with all the children, and we took it in turns to sing Croatian and English songs. There were a number of people who had been coming out to us with lorries full of aid on a regular basis. Not only did they go to the trouble of collecting the stores, they also had all the effort of packing, preparing all the paperwork, organizing the transport, loading everything up, driving for several days and dealing with customs officials at various international borders who often kept them waiting for hours. A man called John Redwood, for instance, a fruit farmer with his own truck, had been out ten times by the time of the opening, and was there for the ceremony. Without the help of people like John and Tony Pratt, who runs an electronics company, and many, many others, life would be taking much longer to come back to Croatia. I do not think people on the receiving end appreciate the enormous effort and personal sacrifice of such amazingly kind and sincere people.

Towards the end of the project we had found that a few people were beginning to question why we were spending so much money on one home. In Finland, for instance, some objections were raised in the media by a couple of journalists who had been out to see the home while I wasn't there and consequently they had not been fully briefed. Their comments made life very hard for Hanna Nurmi at the Finnish Refugee Council, who wanted to raise some money for us. However, after numerous letters going back and forth she was able to raise several thousand pounds, despite the opposition. Our success, in some ways, was our enemy. People who came out to Lipik looked around at all the destruction in Croatia and would ask if there were not causes with more urgent need of a million pounds than the orphanage. Did it need to be quite such a splendid edifice when all around was still ruins?

My answer was always the same. I was not saving lives today but building for the future to give the children hope. I could not justify it on grounds of urgency. The children had not been starving, or even homeless. They were being perfectly well looked after in Selce and were decently clothed and fed. There were many other organizations trying to save lives all over Croatia and Bosnia. I wanted to show people that it was possible to rebuild their lives, that there was no need to despair. The original building had stood for a hundred years. If our building stands for that long it will be a home to thousands of children. I did not want to build something just for today, something cheap and quick and practical. I wanted to build something for the future, something which could be the new symbol of Lipik now that the Kursalon and Fontana were destroyed, and I believe that we succeeded in doing that. The new home had also become a good example of international co-operation working at its best.

Marina and I were also very anxious that it should be as close to a true home as possible, rather than an institution. Each of the main buildings was divided up into a total of seven apartments, and we had imagined each apartment working like a small family group within the larger community. We wanted a mix of ages and genders in each group, just like you would get in a normal family of brothers and sisters, with a teacher acting as a mother or father figure to each group. Each 'family' would then, in our dream, be able to keep dogs, cats, chickens and whatever else they wanted, just like a normal family. In reality it has not yet worked out quite like that, and the boys have been housed in one building while the girls are in the other. Marina and I were also keen for the rooms to be very comfortable with soft furnishings and things that would make them seem like normal homes. We had not managed to achieve that by the opening. The tiled floors and pristine white walls made for elegant rooms rather than homely ones, and there were tables and chairs in the sitting rooms, making them more like classrooms.

Goran never completely agreed with us on these sorts of matters. 'Mark,' he would often say, 'you do not understand, these are not normal children. They mostly come from very disturbed backgrounds and have suffered intense emotional experiences. They can't be treated like children in normal families. This is an institution, not a private home, you must understand that.'

To me the children were always delightful, laughing, teasing and full of fun. Perhaps, because I could not understand what they were saying for most of the time, they seemed to me more angelic than they actually were. They always appeared to need so much love and attention and I felt very inadequate to provide it all. I would spend hours playing ping-pong or football with the bigger boys, or being climbed over and mauled by Stanko and the other little ones, leaving Marina to delve into their minds and help with their social problems. I had a feeling that the traumatic experiences that the children had been through, such as seeing their parents killed before their eyes, gave them the potential to grow up into either very good or very bad adults. Which way they went, I felt, depended on how they were treated by the world for the rest of their childhoods. If they were brought up with love, feeling and understanding, they might even benefit from the terrible experiences they had gone through.

A German aid organization from Westphalia had built some very comfortable, wooden pre-fabricated houses in the town for people who had lost their homes. As a result I had met the Acting German Ambassador, Dr Ellner, on several occasions, and he had expressed his interest in helping us in some way. He was one of the other guests appearing with me on the television show in Zagreb when Snoopy escaped from the audience.

A few months later, when I was in England, I received a telephone call from a Dr Dieter Reithmeier, the General Secretary of the Bavarian Teachers' Union (the BLLV). He had heard from the ambassador about our story. Every year at Christmas his union collected money in the schools of Bavaria for one or two selected charities. The previous year they had collected nearly 600,000 Deutschmarks for charities in Croatia and Bosnia. He wanted to do the same again this year and thought the orphanage might be something they could support. I was very enthusiastic and offered to go to see him in Munich immediately. Having had so many people make offers and then back out at the last minute, I knew it was important to go to him to get a commitment. I flew straight out there, showed him some pictures and told him the story. He said he thought they would like to support us and asked me to write an article about the orphanage. I did as he asked, he published the article in the BLLV magazine and collected 170,000 Deutschmarks for us.

In the spring Dr Reithmeier drove down from Munich to visit us to see how we intended to spend the money. When he arrived and I showed him around the buildings he said very little, none of the usual exclamations of wonder which I was used to from visitors, and he kept asking incisive questions about the children's education, the systems, their welfare and what there was for them to do. No one else had asked such questions before and he was the first person to take the buildings for granted. He could see they were fine but what he was interested in was what was happening inside to teach and stimulate the children, to build their personalities and make them into happy, balanced adults.

This was a surprise to me initially, but I knew exactly what he meant. We had been concentrating on the refurbishment of the buildings so single-mindedly that we had not devoted enough time to thinking about where the children's lives were going to go after that. Because we had been successful in raising money they were being given everything, a nice home, sports facilities, toys, clothes, but it was all just arriving in lorries and they were not actually participating in any creative processes themselves. Whereas I had been expecting to talk to Dr Reithmeier about our need for soft furnishings to make the apartments more homely, he wanted to talk about the possibility of getting hold of some land which the children could use to grow things. He wanted to talk to the staff about the importance of helping the children to develop as people. Now that we had succeeded in putting a roof over the children's heads again, he felt that we should be concentrating our efforts on stimulating their minds and creative talents.

This was like music to my ears. Right from the beginning, as I have said, Marina and I wanted this to be a real home with the normal things that a happy family has and does together. The children had suffered and experienced so much at such an early age, but with love and the right treatment they could actually benefit from their suffering. Dr Reithmeier's visit enthused me – his was a very positive suggestion and a great step forward on the project. The importance of what he had to say was not lost on any of us and we agreed there and then to do something about it.

Now that the buildings were there, and the money was nearly all in, my role was virtually over beyond playing host to people like Dr Reithmeier. There were still some administrative details to take care of, and Goran always seemed pleased to have me around, but he had to get on with the day-to-day job of running the place. He had been confirmed as the full-time director now, but never seemed to have much time to stop and think about anything. As well as having to cope with his own problems at home, like the continuing lack of water, he spent a lot of his time in the car taking children from the home to various places and attending meetings.

The sure and steady rebuilding of Lipik, which had begun with the orphanage and which the ambassador had talked about in his speech, started to speed up in the spring. As I went for walks around the town, piles of bricks and tiles donated by an Italian organization, ISCOS, appeared on the roads outside houses, and more people returned and started to repair their homes and lives. I like to think that at least some of that activity was inspired by what had happened with the children's home, that people felt encouraged by the possibilities of what could be achieved, even when everything looked hopeless.

23

Becoming a Local Monument

Santa Claus came to call at the orphanage on Christmas Eve and Marina and I took some of the children to celebrate Midnight Mass in the makeshift church in the hospital. The centuries-old church in the village had been flattened, and the only part of it which had survived the attack was the bell, which the locals had rehung from a gallows-like structure on the site. It was raining and we all went to church in Dan's Van, which added to the excitement.

I had told the Croatian Government that following on from Lipik, I was keen to help them with another suitable project. On Boxing Day Marina and I left Lipik to fly to Split, as guests of the Government, to look at another possible project there.

We were taken to an old school which was a temporary home for about a hundred mentally handicapped people who had lost their original home in the war. I had not had previous experience with such people, but I found them warm and loving, and we spent two days there with the dynamic director, Maksim Roman, discussing his plans. He had obtained some land in an old olive grove and he wanted to build a new home on it and provide work on the farm for his people. It was a wonderful idea and I would have loved to help and work with him on it, and it would also have given me a job to do in Croatia. Having thought about it for a few days, however, I had to conclude that much as I would have liked to help, I was not convinced that I would be able to get the same support for those people as for the children in Lipik. I very much regretted that I could not give myself to a cause, however worthy, in which I was not confident that I could succeed.

Marina and I went to Mostar for New Year, fifteen months after our last visit when the Serbs were attacking and the Muslims and Croats were fighting together to defend it. Now the Croats were fighting against the Muslims with the Serbs as spectators on the surrounding hills. Marina's parents' flat was now one street back from the front line. Despite the destruction I was surprised to find that there was no despair and life was going on in a remarkably normal way. I met an aunt of Marina's, a comfortable lady in her fifties, who had fled twice from her village in the past year, once from the Serbs and then from the Muslims. Both times she had to swim across the river to escape.

At midnight on New Year's Eve all three sides in the war started to celebrate the New Year with a cacophony of gunfire. I stood mesmerized on the balcony as they fired every weapon they possessed in the town and the surrounding hills. It was like being in the middle of an orchestra made up entirely of drums, playing Tchaikovsky's 1812 Overture.

There was a lot that I liked about this new life. I liked the simplicity of it. There was nothing to buy, so you did not spend any time on shopping. You went out for a loaf of bread and perhaps some eggs and bacon if they were available, and then you went straight home. It contrasted strongly with the trips to the supermarket which are such a basic part of life in England, with the problems of parking the car, choosing from the dazzling displays of goods, and then, worst of all, paying for the mountains of purchases. In Lipik life was at its simplest and most basic. Marina and I were luckier than most in that we did have a roof over our heads, power to warm ourselves and running water. We could also afford to eat in the café if we wanted to.

On the other hand there were many things about living in Croatia, with its bureaucracy left over from Communist days, which were incredibly frustrating. If you want to draw some money out in England you just go to the wall of a bank and punch in some numbers. In Croatia, if I wanted money I would have to go into the bank and it would take five people to complete the transaction, each passing pieces of paper to the next. I would actually get the money from the fifth person about three-quarters of an hour after coming in. On those occasions when I wanted Deutschmarks they actually wrote down the serial number of every note they gave me because they were trying to control inflation and keep a track on the money in circulation.

Whenever I spoke to Caroline on the phone she was always so gentle, kind and forgiving. It must have been so hard for her to restrain her full emotions and not betray her anger on the phone. In fact, I came to look forward to our conversations. It was a relief to be able to talk to some-one in my own language and know that she understood all the nuances of what I was saying, that she understood my sense of humour, my irony and my teasing. I missed her, the boys and my old life horribly. I tried not to call them too much over Christmas, as Caroline had asked me not to, but I needed to send them faxes on several occasions. On one of these it took a particularly long time for them to press the receive button and I was able to hear the sound of carols being sung by King's College Choir in Cambridge. It had always been my favourite part of Christmas and made me very homesick. Only later did I discover that every time the telephone rang during that week Caroline and the boys immediately switched the carols on in a deliber-ate, and successful, attempt to remind me of what I was going to be losing if I stayed on in Lipik. Caroline also used to send me cuttings from my favourite newspapers and magazines.

While I had been away in England Snoopy's ears had got into a terribly matted state. One brisk, bright Sunday morning Snježana and I took him out into the park to tidy him up. We sat down on one of the bullet-scarred and shrapnel-twisted seats with a comb and a pair of scissors. I began hacking away mercilessly as Snoopy struggled to be free of Snježana's powerful grip and we both cooed at him in an attempt to calm him down as his clogged golden locks fell to the ground.

A local man who acted as a guide to visitors appeared from the hospital with a group of tourists. They began to stroll up the path between the little hedges towards us. As he came I could hear his patter: 'This is the Fontana, which was once the symbol of Lipik but is now dry, and that is the Kursalon, which was the centre of life in the town, and that is Colonel Cook . . .' There was a discreet clicking of cameras as the visitors recorded all these sad relics to show their families and friends back home, including the old colonel sitting on the park bench whispering sweet nothings to a cocker spaniel. While it is nice to be known and to have one's achievements noted, the realization that I had in fact become something of a human monument made me think.

In my naivety I thought that when I finally made up my mind to stay in Lipik with Marina and the children, that would be an end to the agonies of my previous indecision. I soon found that this was not to be the case.

The longer I stayed in Lipik, the more involved I became with the children and the people of the village, but at the same time the more clearly I could see that I would have to find something to do there. Although I still could not communicate well with anyone, everyone in the village knew who I was and greeted me cheerfully, but it still was not home. There is always a feeling of comradeship in any community which has been through bad times, like a war or a natural disaster, but I wasn't really part of that because I had not been through the suffering with the people of Lipik. I had not been driven from my home, or had relatives and children murdered or raped. I had not been dispossessed or seen my town destroyed around me. If anything, I had gained an extraordinary experience from my association with Lipik, and lost only what I had chosen to lose by my own behaviour. Goran and the others used to marvel at my apparent determination to return to Lipik again and again, when they were all hoping to find ways of escaping. My main role now seemed to be looking after Snoopy's needs, walking him in the park and around the village, and scrounging food for him in doggy bags after meals at Number Two and the orphanage kitchen.

I received a very thoughtful letter from William over the fax one day in which he showed me even more clearly just how much I was risking losing if I decided to remain in Croatia. I had to go to London for a meeting and met up with him while I was there. He told me in no uncertain terms that if I was to leave his mother I should not expect to see him again either.

The next evening Caroline and I met at a friend's house in London and I armed myself with a bottle of champagne and several large bunches of flowers. We spent several happy evenings together before I returned to Lipik, certain now that I would eventually return to England but still not sure how to do it.

Marina seemed to be as tense as I was about the future. Now that she appeared to have her illness under control she decided that she was going to Zagreb to specialize in rehabilitative medicine. She seemed to take it for granted that I would go back there with her. Despite the improvements in her health, she was still not allowed to go out into the sun, and was told that she probably never would be able to again, which was very upsetting for her as she loved outdoor pursuits. I also found this terribly frustrating. The tension continued to mount and this was particularly evident during the visits of several people who came out from England to see me. These visits took up a lot of my time, which upset Marina as she was not getting my undivided attention, as she wanted. She admitted to me at the time that she was very jealous of all my friends and even of my friendship with Snoopy.

Now that life was returning to Lipik Marina seemed to have more and more to do each day while I had less and less. Despite our joint achievement, we had no common goal for the future. At one stage I thought that we could go and live together in Zagreb while she was doing her medical training. Perhaps I could go to college to learn Croatian, which would make me very well qualified to join some sort of humanitarian aid organization operating in the area. But I realized that for me, going back to school was not the answer.

One morning as I was walking through the park with Snoopy, going from the flat to the orphanage, I knew in my heart that I could not stay in Croatia for ever. I had kept my promise and I now had no real role. I was becoming too attached to the children and it was time for me to go before I became a bore or an embarrassment or both. It had been the most overwhelming emotional experience and I was sad and frightened at the prospect of leaving. I sat on an old park bench as the woodpeckers ate their breakfast noisily above my head. I was desperately sad and shed a tear as Snoopy ran and jumped gleefully around in the undergrowth.

After a few minutes I continued the walk and went straight to my office so that no one would see me. There was a quiet knock on the door and Zdravko, a handsome Romany boy, came in and handed me a card, took my hand, gave me a hug and walked out. He said nothing, which was unusual for him. He was the youngest of six boys and his brothers were now all in jail for serious crimes. He had in fact run away from the orphanage several times to visit them. He was a lovely child, desperate for friendship and love. I looked down and saw that he had given me an old Christmas card with a picture of children on a sledge. I opened it up and inside were written the words 'Jesus loves us, whoever we are. Jesus can wipe away tears. Jesus is our hope and our salvation.' Zdravko does not speak any English and could not have understood what was written there. Why he brought that card to me then in such a quiet, dignified, spiritual way I do not know. Perhaps God was at last showing me the right path.

One day Marina and I had to drive a visitor back to the airport. We were late setting off and as we approached Zagreb there was an ominous clang from under the car, which turned out to be the exhaust pipe falling off, but we continued to scrape and grind our way on. Lights started to flash on and off on the dashboard with no apparent logic. We drove away from the airport slowly and in silence, as if knowing that we had come to the end of the book and did not want to turn the last page. After an hour I pulled off the road and we sat facing the hills, Croatian territory now occupied by Serbs. As the red sun slid behind the hills we decided that our story was finished and we should continue our lives separately. As dusk fell we drove the last few miles back to Lipik through the ruined villages. A red light waved us down at a roadblock. Two policemen checked our papers, including the now very outdated UN pass which I was still gaily using, with the date conveniently obscured to get me through situations like this, and made us get out of the car. Once again we were shown the headlamp that was not working and we expressed our horror and surprise at this revelation. What they did not know was that the brakes in the car had now seized as well. They ticked us off, told us to get the light fixed and gave us back our papers.

'Well,' I said as we drew out, 'what can you expect from a car that was made by Serbs?' We both laughed with relief and the tension of the day evaporated.

I did not leave Lipik immediately. Having decided what I was going to do I felt relieved, but sad at the imminent parting. Marina, Marino the Mayor, Goran and I had one last meeting to discuss further what would be done with the money donated by Dr Reithmeier. The plan on which we decided is to make the home a nucleus for the town, a centre of life for all the children in Lipik, spending 70,000 Deutschmarks of the dona-tion on projects to give them some interest in life, things that they can all do. The bigger boys already had a basketball court which attracted children from the neighbourhood, but other things were needed for the girls and the smaller boys. I drew up a list of activities such as arts, drama, computing, pottery, photography, music, fishing, and the equipment to do these.

A few days before I left, Crown Prince Hassan of Jordan returned for another visit, accompanied by his nephew, the King's son, who is a colonel in their Special Forces. Their entourage consisted of about 100 vehicles, many bristling with machine-guns. They were two hours late and the children's excitement mounted with every passing minute. Marino, who was meant to meet him, had to go off to another important appointment, so Marina stood in for him, which pleased her enormously. It was also very appropriate, as the line-up to meet the Prince now consisted of Marina, Goran and me. The team.

I had Silvester, the smallest and newest child in the home, in my arms. He said something to me and Marina and Goran laughed. 'He wants to know,' Marina translated, 'if the Prince is going to come on a white horse.'

Silvester had come to us with his bigger sister Ivana after their father was killed and their mother died of cancer. After they had been with us for a few days I complimented Ivana on the care she took of her impish little brother. She looked at me with large, sad eyes and explained, 'But he is all I have now.'

The Prince was as wonderful as he had been on the first visit when he was clambering over the rubble right at the beginning of the project. The reason he was two hours late was because he always insists on stopping to talk to everybody he meets on his visits, and this he did with us. He shook hands with every child and teacher in the line from the car park to the house. Before he arrived some of his staff had come with enormous boxes of presents which he had brought over in his plane from Jordan, including two small billiard tables and hundreds of wonderful games. Without the children seeing, we had laid these out upstairs in the playroom. We took the Prince along the line of children and into the sun room, where he signed the visitors' book and looked at photographs of his last visit. Then we went up to the playroom, where he gave his wonderful presents to the children, who were now almost bursting with excitement.

Two days later I returned to England, leaving Lipik for the last time. On my return I found a letter from the headmaster of my old prep school inviting me to present prizes at Speech Day. In my day he had been the history master. 'I well remember your prowess in history,' he wrote, 'and your total inability to recall dates and events. Don't reproach yourself if you have not learnt much history, you have done better by making it.'

Epilogue

When I returned to England I felt intensely aware of the pain and hurt I had caused Caroline and of how badly I had treated her. I was determined to rebuild our lives, heal the wounds and ensure that we regained our love for each other. I knew this would not be easy but, with time, I was confident that we could not only save our marriage but have a stronger one in the end.

We went away to stay with a friend for a quiet weekend in Cornwall and while there I read *Natasha's Story*, Michael Nicholson's moving account of how he rescued a little girl from the orphanage in Sarajevo. As I lay awake that night wrestling with my memories and my conscience, it suddenly became clear to me what we should do next: rebuild the children's home in Sarajevo.

We went to see Michael Nicholson and met Natasha, so young and so happy in her new life. 'What,' I asked Michael, 'about all those children who were left behind?' As I had suspected and hoped, he too wanted to do something for them but did not know what or how. So we decided on a plan to get Caroline and me into Sarajevo to see for ourselves what had happened to them.

Before the war, over 150 children had been living in the home. In the constant shelling of Sarajevo, the children spent endless days and nights in the dark, damp cellars, and their home took eleven direct hits. Several children were wounded. At an early stage a humanitarian organization arranged two convoys to evacuate some of the children to safety. The first, with forty-eight children between four and twelve years old, got through unscathed and went on to Italy. The second convoy, with babies as young as twenty days and children up to four years, was shot at and two children were killed. Their bus was then stopped at a Serbian checkpoint and nine children were taken off and have never been seen again. The rest of the children eventually arrived in Germany.

As the war progressed, the children's home also became home for 400 refugees and was badly vandalized by them: anything, including the wooden floorboards, was burnt to provide warmth, and fittings were removed and sold for food. There are now forty-six children living in the damaged home, including eight babies, two of whom lost both their parents in the war.

Caroline and I have now undertaken to repair this home, to give hope to the children still living there and to enable those who were evacuated to Italy and Germany to return. I am greatly indebted to Hamish Hamilton for agreeing that a royalty from every copy of this book which is sold will help to make this possible.

But then I thought, 'Why only Sarajevo?' There must be thousands of children all over the world who need homes. Man's inhumanity to man has resulted in orphaned children in so many countries without much hope for a future. Again, that word hope comes in. Without a home, what hope have they got? So why not start a new charity to provide children in need with hope and a home? Hope and Homes for Children.

It was at the Royal Albert Hall in 1919 that Miss Eglantine Jebb launched the Save the Children Fund after a visit to the Balkans, where she had been horrified by the plight of the children who had been orphaned and made destitute in the First World War. Was it yet another coincidence that, following my own experiences in the Balkans seventy-five years later, I too was invited to speak at the Royal Albert Hall? I took the opportunity in June, when addressing the Townswomen's Guild in the presence of HRH The Princess Royal, who is President of Save the Children Fund, to launch Hope and Homes for Children.

The aim of this new charity is, as the name clearly says, to provide homes for children who have nowhere to live and to give them hope for the future. We all need somewhere we can call home, and for those of us who are fortunate enough always to have had one it is difficult to imagine what it must be like for a child with nowhere to live. What chance have such children got for a happy or decent life? Hope and Homes for Children will complement the excellent work already done by Save the Children, Feed the Children and other such organizations whose primary aim is to keep children alive and healthy.

When conflict breaks out in any country, the only people affected who are indisputably innocent are the children. Whereas wars are often caused, fuelled and fought by the inbred hatred of adults, it cannot possibly be the fault of the children. If it is possible to help just some of these young and totally innocent victims of conflict, to give them the security of a loving home, then, hopefully, they will be ambassadors for peace in the future.

As I have discovered in the last two years, there are many wonderful, caring and loving people in this world who really do care and want to help others who are less fortunate than themselves. These people give so much of their time, energy and money to the many organizations that help those in need. I trust that some of them will now help me to provide Hope and a Home to children who have neither. Having spent the last thirty-three years in the army, I feel now that my life's mission is just starting.

List of Donors

Below is a list of some of those many people and organizations who helped to make the dream of the Lipik Home come true. I regret very much that it may not be 100 per cent accurate and I may have missed off some whose names should be included. I offer these people my very sincere apologies and ask them to forgive my inefficiency. I would be glad to hear from anyone I may have offended.

Abbey House, Sherborne Boys' School
Mrs P. F. Allen
All Saint's Church, Steeple Langford
Alwen Hough Johnson Ltd
K. M. Amory
Hugo Anson
The Anton Jurgens Charitable Trust
Brian Aris
Eve Arnold
Sven Arnstein
The Rt Hon. Paddy Ashdown, MP
Robin Ashe
Mrs Sarah Aylen

Stephen Back
Kaya Bakalić
Bank of Scotland
Eileen and Den Bark
Sally Bazeley
Bayerischer Lehrer- und Lehrerinnenverband (BLLV)

T. A. Bayley
BBC
BBC Radio Lincolnshire Children in Need Appeal
Mr Beale
K. I. Beard
Robert Beard
Anthea Bell
Jeanne Bell
Martin Bell
Nigel Benn
Fuzzy Bennie
Stephen Benson
Julian Beynon
Black and Decker
Pete Blundell
Colin and Delia Bolden
Mr and Mrs G. Bosman
Marjorie Bosman
Alan Bottomley
Richard Boulton
Braeside Preparatory School
Branston Cubs
Caro and Tony Brewster
N. H. Brighouse

British Airways Authority
British Gas, Lincoln
British Origami Society
British Steel
Mr and Mrs M. Brooks
Mrs Lorraine Bryan
BSB Dorland
Mr and Mrs A. Bulpin
Mrs Jean Bunn
Mrs Joyce Burgess
Stephen Burgess
Patrick and Kathleen Burke
Mrs Hazel Burnett
Miss Butler

Camden Graphics
Cargilfield School
Lady Carnegie
Hilary Carrington
The Rt Hon. Baroness Chalker
   of Wallasey
Emma Charles
Mrs D. Checkland
Chun Wah Lo
Nigel Clarke
Miss Clintworth
Clyde Submarine Base
M. R. and C. G. Compston
Pauline Conway
Major Nick Cook
Mrs Odette Cook
Roger Cook
E. A. and J. E. Cooper
The Coopers' Company and
   Coborn School
Mrs B. Cottam
Croatia Airlines
Mrs D. Curtis
Mario and Ankiza Cvirn

Daily Express

Daily Mail
Mrs Margaret Danby
Erwin Danter
Bill and Kay Dawson
Anne Dixon
Terence Donovan
Brian and Maureen Douglas
   and supporters in New
   Zealand
S. Downie
John Downing
Paula Dumas-Rimmel
P. Dunderdale
Tony and Alex Durie
Zvonimir Džapa

Eastern Daily Press
Jenny Eastwood and supporters
Marika Edge
Jonathan and Gilly Edwardes
Arthur Edwards
Kathy Eldon
Alison and Chris Ellis
Dr Claude Robert Ellner
Lee Eng
Betty Everill
Eversley Preparatory School
George Eykyn

Mohammed Al-Fayed
Lieutenant-Colonel and Mrs J.
   Fillingham
The Finnish Refugee Council
Peter Fitzpatrick
Fortesqueue's Hospitality
   Agents
Fosse Way Primary School
Jane Frost

Tony Gallagher
Mary Garrard

Mr M. Gascoigne-Pees
R. Gay
Janette Gayland
Mr and Mrs P. O. Gershon
Mrs R. A. Glentworth
Phillida Goad
Revd Peter Godden and St
    Hugh's Church
Elisabeth Gotto
Mrs H. Gray
Mladen Grbin
Anna Green
Deirdre Green
Miss K. Groves
Brian Gunton
10th PMO Gurkha Rifles

Pamela Haigh
Hall Grove School
Ray Hamilton
Miss B. C. Hannay
Majella Haran
Ros Hardie and supporters
David Harding (in memory of
    his father)
Mrs S. Harris
Brenda Harrison
Michael and Joanna Harrison
His Royal Highness Crown
    Prince Hassan Bin Talal of
    Jordan
Mark Hatt-Cook
Hawker Siddeley Power Plant
    Ltd
Pru and David Hawkins
The Henderson family
Barbara Heydon
Hickling and Squires
Gloria Hobday
Mr and Mrs Keith Hopkins
Robert Horne

Mr M. Horner
Mrs Thelma Horton
House of Fraser
Howitt Printing
Hrvatska Malteska Sluzba
Chris Hughes
Colonel and Mrs Jerry Hunter

Inner Wheel Club of Lincoln
Interkonzalting, Zagreb

Dr and Mrs Johnstone-Jones
Johnstons of Elgin
Sarah Jones

Nony and Sam Kerr-Smiley
Svetislav Kikaš

Dr and Mrs Spiro J. Latsis and
    family
Suganya Lee and supporters in
    Canada
Leslie Leek
A. G. Legner de Lacroix
Letzebuerger Initiativ Fir
    Kroatien
The Leys School
Lord Lichfield
Lincoln Cooperative Society
12th Lincoln Cubs, Scouts and
    Ventures
28th Lincoln Cubs, Scouts and
    Beavers
Lincoln Inner Wheel
Lincoln Inner Wheel Overseas
    Section
Lincoln Theological College
Lincolnshire County Council
Ling Moor County Primary
    School
Mr J. T. Lister

Roy Love
Lune Valley Refugee Aid
Sara Lyle
Mrs S. E. McConnell
Steve McCurry
Miss McDonald
Tony McGee
Martin McInally
Sheila McIver
Neil and Penny McKernow
John MacKinlay
Sir Fitzroy and Lady Maclean
Margaret McLean
Miss E. P. McPeake
Stipe Mandarelo
Manor Leas Junior School,
  Lincoln
G. R. and I. M. Mark
Dawn Martin
Mr and Mrs T. W. Matthews
Ian and Polly Mayman
C. E. Meade
Emma-Louise Merbitz
Miss M. Milner
Mr and Mrs Ming Paul Lee
Moorland County Infant
  School, Lincoln
Miss N. M. Morgan
Franz Mühlbacher of KADA
MacDonald Muir

NADA, Finland
Nationwide Building Society
Netherhampton Harvest Festival Supper
Newburgh Congregational
  Church
Dr Duncan Newton and choir
  group
Mr and Mrs Nichols
Revd J. Nicholson

P. and M. Nolan
North Kesteven School, Lincoln
Mrs Julie Oaks
Terry O'Neill
Martha Ospina
Overseas Development
  Administration
Mr and Mrs Oxley
Rosie Oxley

W. B. Page
Mrs P. A. Pangbourne
Kate Parker and supporters in
  Canada
Elizabeth Paterson
Revd Tony Pepper
Perth Methodist Church
R. G. Philipson
Miss Phipps
Mrs Barbara Pickering
Mrs Lucy Pickering
Hew and Jean Pike
PJP plc
E. S. Plimmer
Helena Posnett
Roger and Fiona Potter
Tony and Jean Pratt
Peter Praxmarer
A. C. Pugh
Helen Pugh

RAF Lyneham
Mrs D. Rafferty
Mr and Mrs D. L. Raine
J. and D. Raine
Esther Rantzen
John and Jenny Redwood
Diether Reithmeier
S. J. Rickard
S. Ripley
Janet Robarts

A. E. Robbins
Richard and Emma Roc
Ivan Rogar
Roger Williams University, USA
Dinah Rose
The Royal School, Dungannon
Denis Rutovitz

St Alphege Church, Aldershot
St Alphege Church, Whitstable
St George's VA School,
  Harpenden
St Luke's Church, Canning
  Crescent
St Lawrence's Church,
  Stellingthorpe
St Margaret's Church, Lowestoft
St Matthew's Church, Oxford
St Michael's Home
Catherine Sampson
Sandox
Sandford Orcas PCC
Saxilby village, near Lincoln
P. J. M. Scott-Moncrieff
Caroline Sharp
Miss J. Sharpe
Mrs Sheldon
Vernon Sheldon
Sherborne Boys' School
Sherborne Girls' School
Ivan Šimunović
Jo Slack
Eric Smallwood
Heather Smart
Mike Smith
Tony and May Smith
Lord Snowdon
Mr and Mrs Bryan Sparrow
Mandy Sprague
Miss P. Stacey
Koo Stark

Mrs M. C. Stebbings
Keith and Pammie Steel
Steeple Langford PCC
Steeple Langford School
Jura Straga
Studio Graph
Sturton and Stour villages, near
  Lincoln
The *Sun*
Miss S. E. Taylor
Sidney and Elvey Taylor
W. L. Taylor
Tom Thirkell
Thorneyholme Hall Health Spa
3M
Mr W. Thursfield
The Tim Burke Memorial Fund
Townsend Hook
Mr Toyne
K. M. Tyle
Tyne Theatre and Opera House

Mrs J. Underwood
Uniparts
United Distillers
United Nations Protection Force
  (UNPROFOR)
A. M. Unwin
Slobodan Urlić

Mrs Vallis
Miss Veasey
Richard and Venetia Venning

Mrs J. Walden
General Sir Walter Walker
Walsall Aid Convoy
The Warden, Orrin Close
Richard G. Ware
Nigel and Lisa Warren
Nigel Washbourne

Andrew and Pippa Watt
Johnny and Di Watts
Miss S. Watts
Mrs Carol Webster
Peter Welby
Wesley's Chapel Leysian Centre
Miss West
Wharton County Primary School
The Willey family
Mr and Mrs C. J. Williams
Mrs G. Williams
Willingham-by-Stow Cubs

Tony and Rosalind Wilson
Alexandra Woodall
Revd Woodhouse
Woolworth's
The Worshipful Company of
   Cutlers

Yeo Vale
Simon Varvill
Tiemen Venema

Marino Zanetti